REIKI
MEDITATIONS
for BEGINNERS

Disclaimer

This book is not intended to treat, diagnose or prescribe. The information contained herein is in no way to be considered as a substitute for a consultation with a duly licenesed health care professional.

Author: Lawrence Ellyard

Copyright © 2010 by Lawrence Ellyard

First Edition 2010
Printed in the United States of America
ISBN: 978-0-9102-6197-5
Formerly Published under ISBN: 978-1-8469-4098-9

LOTUS
PRESS
Published by:
Lotus Press, P.O. Box 325, Twin Lakes, WI 53181 USA
web:www.lotuspress.com
Email:lotuspress@lotuspress.com
800.824.6396

REIKI
MEDITATIONS
for BEGINNERS

The Art of Meditation, the Practice of Reiki

By LAWRENCE ELLYARD

Best Selling Author of
"Reiki 200 Questions and Answers for Beginners"

Foreword by David Vennells
– Author of *'Reiki Mastery'*

LOTUS PRESS

Published by
Lotus Press
P.O. Box 325
Twin Lakes, WI 53181 USA
800-824-6396 (toll free order phone)
262-889-8561 (office phone)
262-889-2461 (office fax
www.lotuspress.com (website)
lotuspress@lotuspress.com (email)

PRAISE FOR

REIKI
MEDITATIONS
for BEGINNERS

One of the few Reiki books which really covers something new and valuable. Reiki and meditation is the core topic for everyone who likes to use Usui-Reiki as a spiritual path. This is why Mikao Usui emphasized so much to meditate every morning and every evening. A must read for every serious Reiki- Practitioner! **Walter Lübeck**, co-author of *The Spirit of Reiki*

Combining Reiki and Meditation can be a wonderful, life-enhancing experience, and this book provides some lovely examples. **Penelope Quest**, best-selling author of *Reiki For Life*

"Reiki Meditations" is an excellent book for Reiki practitioners, meditators, as well as for anyone interested in Reiki or meditation. The basic meditations are very beneficial to bring tranquility to the mind.
I strongly recommend that all Reiki practitioners follow some form of meditation to develop a state of calm and equanimity before Reiki treatments. I enjoyed reading Lawrence's practical and easy to follow book and highly recommend it. **Dr. Ranga J. Premaratna**, Ph.D, Reiki;Jin kei Do Teacher and Head of Lineage

Lawrence Ellyard presents the traditional practices of Mikao Usui, the founder of Reiki, in an easy to follow manner. He also offers invaluable advice for dealing with the initial obstacles which arise in any meditation practice. A must-read for all Reiki practitioners interested in the heart of Usui's legacy, with meditative practices that suport the path to enlightenment. **Dr. Paula Horan**, author of *Empowerment Through Reiki*

This is a good practical book informing the beginner what to consider and how to start meditation. Lawrence gives detailed descriptions about the various aspects of meditation and Reiki practices. Furthermore the reader receives enhanced knowledge on practical points and inspiration for their daily mediation. **Tanmaya Honervogt**, author of *Inner Reiki*

Lawrence Ellyard's "Reiki Meditations For Beginners" offers an appealing variety of meditations, drawn from traditional Japanese Reiki, Buddhism, yoga, creative visualization, and his own inner wisdom, to help readers claim greater peace and healing in their lives. This is a gentle, compassionate work! **Amy Z. Rowland**, author of *Intuitive Reiki For Our Times* and *Traditional Reiki For Our Times.*

This is a useful, practical book invaluable to anyone wishing to deepen their understanding and practice of Reiki and meditation. **Penny Parkes**, Reiki Master and author of *15-Minute Reiki*

CONTENTS

Dealing with Depression

ACKNOWLEDGEMENTS

What I know of Reiki and meditation I know because of my teachers. I therefore wish to express my thanks to all of my teachers both past and present who were willing to share their knowledge and experiences with me. It is with deep respect that I bow down to honour our founder Mikao Usui. Like an early explorer, he mapped a path we all could follow.

My thanks also go to the many Reiki teachers with whom I have studied.

These include Dawn Bruggen; Brian and Carole Daxter; Margot 'Deepa' Slater; Gary Samer; Dr. Richard Blackwell; Franz Stiene; and Dr. Ranga J. Premaratna.

There is also a great deal I have learnt from the written instructions of Reiki authors and teachers. My thanks also go to Walter Lübeck; Frank Arjava Petter; Richard Rivard; Hiroshi Doi; Amy Rowland; Chris Marsh and Adonea for their research and continuing work in this area.

I also wish to thank my Buddhist Masters who have been both living examples and teachers of meditation, including: Lama Ole Nydahl, The Venerable Namgyal Rinpoche, Lama Chime Shore, and His Holiness the 17th Karmapa - Thaye Dorje.

FOREWORD

When Lawrence asked me if I would write a foreword for 'Reiki Meditations for Beginners' I was very happy to say 'yes'! This book, as with all Lawrence's work, is designed to help others. To help and empower others to improve their quality of life through Reiki, Meditation, Wisdom and Love.

Western understanding of Reiki has changed dramatically over the last ten years. Reiki has developed from a little known 'new age therapy' to a very popular well-known and respected complimentary therapy, often used in hospitals and hospices all over the world. But of course it is much more than just a healing therapy. I am constantly delighted to meet people from all backgrounds who have already tried and enjoyed Reiki. It is amazing how comfortable people are with Reiki. Whatever their background or life experiences as soon as they feel Reiki they relax and open up. I have never met anyone who has stood up and said 'oh no I don't like this, this isn't for me'. People like it because it makes them feel good. It makes them feel good in a way that possessions, money and status cannot. It fulfils a deep need for inner peace and happiness that cannot be found by searching in the external world.

No matter how much human beings develop externally it will not bring the inner peace and happiness we wish for. How could it? How can external development bring internal results? Only inner development can bring inner results. Happiness, peace, contentment, joy, empathy, understanding, love are all inner qualities. They are not made of metal or wood or stone. Of course the things we create externally do make our lives a little easier and sometimes bring great benefit. We all need hospitals, schools, roads etc. Such things are necessary for our modern world to function, they can reduce suffering and improve our quality of life. But we can never find a 'final solution' in these things.

If we invest too much time developing externally what happens to our internal world? It simply degenerates. When we value external development over internal development our inner qualities become weaker and weaker. We become more concerned with our own welfare, less patient, more suspicious, more discriminating, less kind and less content. Our desires increase and we need more external stimulus to satisfy our childish mind. It doesn't take a person of great wisdom to see that an emphasis on external development could eventually bring this world to an end.

This book is very special because it is about inner development. Inner development is the essence of meditation. We are all inner beings. We are not naturally external beings; we have just forgotten our nature. We have become so caught up in the external world that we have forgotten what it means to be an inner being, we have forgotten who we are. It is almost as if we have fallen under a spell and now believe that happiness can be found 'outside'. If we can get everything 'outside' just right, the right job, the right partner, the right car we will be happy. Of course the sense of happiness and fulfilment we seek in external things can only be found 'inside'. We need to look within.

What we achieve externally with our life has no great meaning. When our life comes to an end we are separated from all possessions and people. We all have to go through this. Death is certain, we will have to let go of everything. Life also passes quickly, even 70 or 80 years is not a long time. Ask someone who is old and they will tell you that you have no time to waste and that it is important to make the most of life. Thinking like this everyday helps us to focus on what is important and to let go of what is not important. We can take nothing with us when we die, except our inner qualities. This is why it is so important to become an inner being, someone who is trying to develop his or her inner qualities. This book is a great way to start this journey it clearly explains how to begin and progress along the path of meditation and also contains many ideas and techniques for advanced Reiki practitioners.

Reiki, especially when combined with meditation, can help us change inside. It can help us become inner beings and gradually let go of our desire for external development and temporary pleasure. This is a fantastic journey to begin. It is a journey of self-discovery. It is a journey of life. It is about discovering the real meaning of life. It is our inner life that is our real life, it is when we start to look within that our life really begins.

David Vennells, author of *Reiki Mastery and Reiki for Beginners.*

DEDICATION

This book is dedicated to the benefit of all beings everywhere.

INTRODUCTION

Anyone who has ever experienced receiving Reiki will attest to the deeply peaceful result of this gentle healing art. Within a few moments our body and mind slide into a restful yet aware state. It is not uncommon for many people to fall asleep during a Reiki treatment but for those who remain awake many report a state of awareness similar to deep states of meditation. Receiving Reiki has this potential. It is something which is not necessarily reserved for the accomplished long standing practitioner alone. Many people who receive Reiki report these altered states even from the first treatment. We can therefore say that Reiki has a natural power to affect our minds in positive healing ways.

Aside from the results of receiving or giving Reiki, Mikao Usui (Reiki's founder) in his infinite wisdom taught his students many different kinds of meditation practices to assist them in fine tuning their Reiki abilities.

These took the form of the Usui methods for energy meditation. Although Usui was influenced by the various schools of Buddhism of his day, it seems he also drew upon other influences, such as those found in China such as Chi Kung and other esoteric traditions which were increasing popular in Japan in his day. To this end, many of these traditional Reiki practices are presented in this book as well as some modern ones which have been cultivated by dedicated Reiki teachers the world over.

As you leaf through the pages, be mindful that you are not expected to utilise every meditation practice. The great variety is designed to give you options. You may find some practices are more appropriate for your own development than others. Mikao Usui gave different meditations according to his students' abilities and tendencies. This choice is presented here today for Western practitioners.

Many of the meditations presented in this book also draw from my personal experiences and training in Reiki both in the western and Japanese forms, as well as meditations from my study in Tibetan and Hinayana (Southern Schools) Buddhism.

I have been asked for many years to write a more comprehensive book on the practice of meditation and Reiki. To create a source of information in book form where meditations could be explained in greater detail, as well as sharing genuine tools for learning meditation. The result is this book.

The majority of the meditations presented in this book are traditionally given during Reiki workshops however anyone can utilize these meditations and achieve positive results, with or without formal Reiki training. Although formal Reiki training is tremendously beneficial from a reliable Reiki teacher, these meditations open the door for anyone who is interested in getting a taste of Reiki and meditation as well as their potential to bring greater peace and healing into one's life.

As well as teaching the Japanese Reiki meditations in classes, I have also developed many others over the last 15 years of teaching Reiki to hundreds of people from all walks of life. Whether taught formally in Reiki classes or at 'Reiki Share' practice evenings, these meditations have always proven to be a reliable way to experience our minds radiance directly.

In my experience with other Reiki teachers and in re-training many existing Reiki practitioners, more often than not a general misunderstanding of Reiki and meditation is encountered. In many cases, for new and existing students alike, taking a class at our Institute will result in their first real experience of meditation.

In the same way Reiki is passed from Master to Student, so it is that the practices of Meditation are passed. The origins of the Usui Reiki meditations first made their way to the West in 1997 through a German Reiki Master, Frank Arjava Petter. He was responsible for introducing new material from Japan and published a number of Reiki books, including 'Reiki Fire' and 'The Legacy of Dr. Usui'. Later in 1999 through one member of the Usui Reiki Gakkai (Usui's original Reiki society in Japan) Hiroshi Doi began sharing these practices to western trained Reiki Masters.

Originally the Usui Reiki Gakkai was for members only and knowledge of these inner practices remained largely unknown to Western Reiki teachers prior to 1997.

Hiroshi broke with tradition and set about teaching the original Usui meditations to western trained Reiki Masters for the first time.

Until this time, there was little knowledge of an existing Reiki tradition in Japan. Many Western trained Reiki teachers believed that Reiki had died out in Japan during the Second World War. During Usui's life, he trained some 17 teachers to pass on his teachings and many followed his advice. Shortly after he died, the Usui Reiki Gakkai was formed.

The Usui Reiki Ryoho Gakkai, was the first society formed in honour of Mikao Usui. Some speculation still surrounds whether Mikao Usui actually began the society, as he is listed as the first chairperson in 1922. However, it is more likely that this was done as an honorary title out of respect for the legacy which Mikao Usui had left his students.

This society still exists today and there have been six presidents since Mikao Usui:

Mr. Juzaburo Ushida	1865-1935,
Mr. Kanichi Taketomi	1878-1960,
Mr. Yoshiharu Watanabe	(unknown - 1960),
Mr. Hoichi Wanami	1883-1975,
Ms. Kimiko Koyama	1906-1999,

and the current president Mr. Masayoshi Kondo

Research suggests that the second chairperson, Juzaburo Ushida (1865-1935) began the learning society shortly after Usui Sensei's passing in 1926. Ushida was also the author of the Usui Memorial, where Usui's grave memorial rests - at Saihoji temple in the Toyotama district of Tokyo.

During the Second World War, the Reiki Gakkai went underground, moving its headquarters so as not to be detected as being a part of the Japanese peace movement. After the war when things had settled down, the Reiki Gakkai re-grouped and continued its practices formally. Today, the Reiki Gakkai continues its practices and teachings based on Mikao Usui's inspiration.

In the Reiki Gakkai, many techniques are taught to enhance a student's ability to generate spiritual growth; how to heal oneself and others; and to increase awareness of subtle energy. The formal instruction of Reiki in the learning society takes place in a very methodical and progressive manner. The emphasis is on complete accomplishment of each practice before proceeding to a new level. The Gakkai therefore, has ranks and levels within their system.

The Reiki Gakkai is also a closed Reiki Society. They do not encourage contact with foreigners and all members are asked not to discuss the details of their training with those who are not members. The Reiki Gakkai currently consists of 200 members and is based in Tokyo. Students learn on a weekly basis in the society. During these meetings, students chant the Reiki Principles, recite Waka poetry* and practice *Hatsurei-ho* (energy enhancing practices). Each week, Shinpiden (teacher) Sensei's give students regular Reiju (energy empowerments). These regular empowerments act to purify and open the students' energy channels.

Today, variations of this Reiki movement exist under other names, these include: Gendai Reiki (Modern Reiki Healing Method), Usui Reiki Ryoho and Japanese Reiki Method.

The reason for this brief lesson in history relates to a split which occurred in the Reiki Lineage. This was due to one of Usui's last teacher/students. Chuijro Hayashi was a student of Mikao Usui only for a period of 10 months* in 1925, before Usui's passing. *Other sources indicate a longer association. Notably, Hayashi is considered by many modern Reiki teachers to be the only successor of Usui's teachings however, new research clearly differs in this opinion.

Some time in 1925 Hayashi met Mikao Usui and prior to this Chuijro was a commander in the imperial navy, where he also gained training in Western Allopathic and Eastern Chinese Medicine. In June of 1925, Hayashi received his teachers training in Usui's Reiki system. Some sources say that Chujiro Hayashi was also Methodist Christian and as such, did not gain the complete transmission of Usui's Reiki system due to his religious beliefs. However, Hayashi's religious background was confirmed by Mrs. Yamaguchi, a student of Hayashi. She confirmed that he was a Buddhist and was buried in the tradition of the Buddhist way. For all we know, he may have explored several religious traditions at the time.

On March 9th, 1926, Mikao Usui died. Counter to the story promulgated by

*Waka poetry is a traditional Japanese poetic form with fixed line lengths of 5-7-5-7-7 syllables. Much like Haiku poems, Waka poetry expresses spiritual aspirations, which aid in the expression of the Enlightened Mind.

Hawayo Takata (a student of Hayashi), Dr. Hayashi was neither considered, nor chosen as Usui's direct and only successor. Shortly after Usui's passing the Reiki Gakkai was formed and Hayashi was said to be involved with this learning society.

Later in 1931, Dr. Hayashi was also said to have left the society as a result of a dispute with the then chairman of the society, Taketomi Sensei. This may have been due to the significant changes he made to Usui's Reiki system. Hayashi continued to work at Dr. Usui's Reiki clinic, which was called the Usui Memorial Clinic. Hayashi soon renamed the clinic calling it 'Hayashi Reiki Kenkyu kai' or Hayashi Reiki Research Society.

Mrs. Takata inherited Hayashi's system under the Usui name and thus propagated his teachings as the Usui System of Natural Healing. It is now clear that Mrs. Takata made many changes to the teachings of Hayashi. She did not formally begin teaching teachers until the early 1970's.

Because of all these changes and general misinformation, a new student to Reiki will often encounter considerable confusion regarding Reiki lineage and styles.

Ironically, the title 'The Usui System of Natural Healing' or 'Usui Shiki Ryoho', used by Reiki teachers in the west actually indicates the system of Reiki belonging to Mrs. Takata.

Mrs. Takata brought her adapted system of Reiki to America in the beginning of the 1970's and over a 10 year period, taught 22 western students to the teacher level of her system. Many of these students went on to prolifically teach Reiki, notably Phyllis Furumoto *(The Reiki Alliance)*, Barbara Weber Ray *(The Radiance Technique)* as well as many others. As a result of these teachers and others that followed, Reiki spread globally within a few short years. Today, there are literally millions of Reiki practitioners world-wide and their teachings are largely based on what was passed on from Mrs. Takata.

Beyond the information shared through Reiki Masters such as Frank Arjava Petter in 1997, news of a Japanese Reiki teacher caught the imagination and interest of western trained teachers from all over the world. This brings us to the encounter of Hiroshi Doi.

In Vancouver 1999, a seminar was held by Hiroshi Doi for 60 Western trained Reiki Masters and was attended by Reiki teachers from several countries. During the days which followed, many of the original Reiki teachings were passed onto Western trained Reiki Masters for the first time. Word of new Usui techniques and meditations soon spread and within a short time, western trained teachers began using these practices in their own classes.

It was shortly after in the year 2000 that I received these teachings and I set about re-training my existing Reiki students and teachers in the new material. Like myself, my students were deeply impressed with the meditation practices and like several pennies dropping from heaven, many pieces of the Reiki puzzle became realized. For years I had suspected there was more to Reiki than what was being taught through the western lineage. Learning the Japanese style brought completion to that search and brought with it confidence in a complete practice of Reiki.

It is my hope that you will find the practices of both traditional Japanese and others of use in your Reiki practice. Whether you are a beginner or seasoned practitioner or teacher, I encourage you to try the meditations for yourself to see what benefits they bring.

Reiki is as unique as each of us and speaks to us on an individual level. By engaging in these practices, may Reiki speak to you in a sweet voice of healing and deepening your experience of the path of peace.

Lawrence Ellyard.
Byron Bay, New South Wales, Australia- April 2010

PART ONE – ALL ABOUT REIKI

How to use this book

Reiki Meditations for Beginners is for anyone interested in deepening their experience of Reiki and meditation. This book is set out in three parts. Part One offers a general introduction to Reiki and, although not a complete guide to the practice of Reiki (as this is covered in my previous books), it does offer an overview of Reiki.

Part Two explores the practice of meditation as well as how to navigate through the intricacies of our minds. This section covers everything we need to know about establishing a Meditation practice, as well as knowing how to deal with disturbing emotions and how to get the most out of meditation practice. This part also provides an insight into 'Buddhist view' and the nature of reality.

Part Three shares a variety of Reiki meditations both traditional Japanese and non-traditional. Included is a chapter on *Mudras* (hand gestures) with accompanying meditations, as well as meditations to calm and hold the mind. There are meditations for purification and how to transform disturbing emotions. The final chapter describes traditional meditation practices from the Japanese style of Reiki.

It is my hope that reading this book will give you a rounded overview of both Reiki and the practice of meditation and bring your experience of both to higher and lasting levels.

CHAPTER 1

WHAT IS REIKI?

Reiki is a Japanese word meaning Universal Life Force Energy and is a Japanese hands-on healing modality based on the transference of vital energy. The system of Reiki is a complete way of healing that transforms and heals the body and mind. By utilizing the methods within the Reiki system, a Reiki practitioner can transfer healing energy via their hands to anyone or anything. This extends to transferring healing energy in non-local ways, in the form of distance healing.

Anyone can learn Reiki. It is not just for people with a special talent or someone with a God-given ability. In fact, Reiki has nothing to do with 'Gods or Devils' but is a spiritual system that is based on aligning one's energy system with the Universal frequency.

To do Reiki all that is required is a desire to learn and the attunements (initiations) from a qualified Reiki Instructor. Attunement into Reiki is a necessary step, as this allows the alignment to the Reiki frequency. With this alignment, our energy merges with the Reiki energy and we become a conduit or channel, much like a radio being tuned to a station. This energy is then always available and it can be applied for healing effects to numerous situations.

Reiki energy is the healing energy of the Universe. It represents a matrix of non-dualistic energy, which permeates all things. This means it only generates healing, not harm. A Reiki practitioner can harness this vital energy (once attuned to it) and it is often experienced as a warm heat emanating from the palms of the practitioner.

To switch on the Reiki ability, this transmission comes via a Reiki teacher, who is someone trained and experienced in the precise methods for creating this alignment within the practitioner. Much like a formula, the attunement when correctly given will create a positive result. Once this alignment is complete, the practitioner can then use this healing energy in a variety of ways to restore the body, mind and emotions to a harmonious state. Reiki has beneficial results for those who give, as well as those who receive it.

The way Reiki is applied is via the hands. The practitioner places their hands on the corresponding charkas (energy centres), meridians and organs, transferring healing energy to the recipient. Some Reiki styles recommend a set sequence of hand positions whereas other styles recommend a more intuitive approach.

Whichever approach is used, the result of a treatment is a deeply relaxing experience for both the practitioner and the recipient. Anyone who has ever received a Reiki treatment can attest to the deeply meditative state one enters. Within a few short moments after the treatment begins, one's mind, body and emotions abide in a deep and peaceful place.

In order for the recipient to receive Reiki from the facilitator, it is necessary for the Reiki energy to pass through the facilitator and it is for this reason that both receive the benefits of this energy. Unlike other systems of healing and bodywork, where a practitioner can feel somewhat drained or depleted, Reiki only serves to replenish and increase one's vitality and general feeling of well-being.

During a Reiki treatment, no movement is required, nor is it necessary to remove clothing or to fix the mind in deep focus to achieve healing effects. Some of the immediate benefits from a treatment are reduced stress, inner peace and deep rest.

Reiki incorporates a number of practical healing techniques, which are easy and effective in their application and method.

Reiki is also an excellent technique for stress management, as well as being a complementary treatment to western allopathic medicine. The transference of Reiki energy actually increases the bodies natural ability to heal itself. When we consider that energy is the foundation of all life, it makes sense that if we have more energy constantly available to us, we will gradually enhance our health and personal well-being.

Learning Reiki

Learning Reiki, for the most part, usually takes the form of a workshop. Here, an experienced Reiki teacher passes on both their experience and knowledge regarding the system of Reiki. During a class (which is usually held over two consecutive days) the participants learn a variety of new skills for healing themselves and others.

In a First Degree or Beginners seminar, both self-healing and facilitating healing for others is taught and practised. This usually involves a series of hand positions and additional methods for being able to intuitively sense where the

Reiki energy is required.

Another component of most Reiki workshops, (as styles and methodology varies from one system to the next), is the practice of Reiki meditations. For example, in the Japanese style of Reiki, a series of meditations are presented to assist new students in cultivating a deep awareness and understanding of the energy, as well as how to actively enhance and increase one's healing ability.

The third component of a Reiki workshop is the Reiki attunements. This is when the Reiki teacher awakens or activates the students healing ability via a short ritual which is given as part of the Reiki teachings. I will go more into attunements in the section which follows.

To summarize, to become a competent and skilful practitioner of Reiki, one requires methods; transmission, (which takes the form of the Reiki attunements) and experience both in the form of meditation practice and through hands-on treatments.

The Reiki Lineage

A 'Reiki lineage' describes the family tree of Reiki teachers and their students, dating back to the founder, Mikao Usui. When we think of a lineage in Reiki we can think a Reiki lineage is much like an ancestry of those who have previously walked the path of Reiki. We could say that our own ancestry, such as our parents and grandparents and our great, great grandparents are part of our family lineage. Just in the same way, a Reiki lineage represents our spiritual Reiki ancestry.

To illustrate an example, one well-known Reiki lineage is that of Mrs. Takata. Mrs. Takata was responsible for bringing Reiki to the west for the very first time to America in the early 1970's. Her lineage or family tree goes like this: Usui; Hayashi; and Takata. In this example, Hayashi was a student of Usui. Later, Hayashi became a teacher in his own right and in time began to teach his own students. One of his students was Mrs. Takata, who received attunements into Reiki and finally became a teacher in her own right. She in turn began to teach her own students, some of whom became teachers of her system. And so the lineage grows with each generation of Reiki teacher.

There are of course many other Reiki lineages, some are many teachers long and some of the methods *(depending upon the teachers in those lineages)* have changed or the Reiki teachings have been adapted. Subsequently, information may change from teacher to teacher and as a result, the transmission may also weaken. On the other hand, there are some Reiki lineages which have remained unchanged over many decades in Japan, giving students the opportunity to learn a more traditional and original Reiki style.

When a student receives a Reiki attunement, a connection to the lineage of the Reiki teacher is conferred. The student's Reiki lineage is in place from that point on. One then usually inherits the teachings and transmission of this lineage, with instruction via the Reiki teacher.

A Reiki teacher or, as is often described, a *'Reiki Master'*, has the ability to give a transmission and to pass on the lineage of their teacher's tradition. Whereas a practitioner can give Reiki to another, they cannot pass on the Reiki transmission which takes the form of the Reiki Attunements.

It is for this reason that having a Reiki lineage is so important. Having a teacher who has the correct transmission and methods is also very important. This is because they carry the ability to awaken and transmit the power of the lineage and methodology of Reiki.

For example, you cannot really learn Reiki as such from a book. All you get is information but not transmission. You need a living teacher who can pass on the tradition via the Reiki attunements. Without this your Reiki ability cannot be activated.

The Reiki Attunements

The Reiki attunements are the energy alignments a teacher of Reiki gives to their student. In various schools and styles of Reiki the ways these attunements are given to the student vary in approach and methodology. However, irrespective of differences in methodology, in most cases each attunement activates an ability to use Reiki energy for oneself and others almost immediately.

If we were to use an analogy of what an attunement is, then we might think that the Reiki energy is a radio signal, our energy body a radio and our radio antenna or receiver the body's energy system. When a teacher adjusts our antenna (by tuning in our dials or energy centers) we effectively pick up the station 'Reiki' and as a result, any previous static that was found on our station is removed and a clear reception is found. Thus, the ability to channel Reiki energy is bestowed.

The actual Reiki attunement is a small ceremony, which creates this alignment.

Many attunement procedures make use of Reiki symbols particular to the system and these are drawn by the teacher into various places of energy flow in the recipient's body. The symbols act like keys. Much like opening a door, these symbols open new pathways of energy, which were previously laying dormant or 'locked up' in the person's energy system.

The beginners Reiki level consists of four separate Reiki Attunements. Each attunement is given gradually over two days. Like gradually turning on a light with a dimmer switch, each attunement opens the students Reiki ability. By the fourth Reiki attunement the light is on and radiates at full capacity.

Another way to describe the Reiki attunement is like a chemical formula. Provided we have the correct formula we will have the desired result. If we change the formula we get a different result. For example the chemical formula H_2O uses the formula for water: two hydrogen and one oxygen molecule. But if we change that formula to H_2O_2 we get hydrogen dioxide. In this analogy we have a small change in the formula and a big change in the result.

So, it is important to have the correct transmission from a qualified teacher of Reiki. Today, there are many books that have published Reiki attunements. This is all well and good, but if the reader does not have the Reiki attunement from a qualified teacher of the same tradition and lineage then having this information is of little use. You could think of it like having a car and putting in petrol only to realize that you do not have any keys to start the car.

Publishing the Reiki attunement procedures is a little bit like this. However, if you do have the Reiki attunements via a qualified teacher you also receive the keys for that car enabling you to drive down the path to healing.

Traditional and Non-traditional Reiki

Traditional Reiki is considered to be the styles or systems of Reiki which have an uninterrupted line of teachings from the founder, Mikao Usui. Other characteristics include teachers who pass on this tradition in a similar manner, and thirdly, a continuity of practice, methodology and understanding of the material. These points are supportive in determining the style or tradition of Reiki. When a teaching departs from these components, the system changes and either becomes a new system or style and therefore becomes a new Reiki style.

It is most important to make clear distinctions where changes are made within Reiki.

One should also be aware that the majority of the Reiki styles available today have already been combined with other systems of healing and religion. In other cases Reiki styles have been invented or created out of various teachers' insights, as well as from various channelled material.

Meditation Practice and Reiki

The original teaching of Reiki as taught by Reiki's founder, Mikao Usui had a strong emphasis placed on meditation and he taught several practices to his students before his death in 1926. Usui considered the path of Reiki as a complete system for liberation with healing being a by-product or benefit upon the way to enlightenment. Therefore the practice of meditation was high on the agenda for those who wished to develop upon the Reiki path. The practice of your Reiki and meditation are certainly synonymous with one another. You cannot do Reiki without experiencing a heightened state of awareness and meditation. Of course some people choose to focus purely on Reiki without meditation for it does work without our mental focus (provided you have received the Reiki Attunements from a qualified Reiki teacher), but to achieve the complete benefits of a Reiki treatment, the focus of the practitioner certainly enhances the overall experience.

If we were to measure the brain waves of an experienced Reiki practitioner whilst giving a Reiki treatment, we would find that their brain waves are of a similar state to deep meditation. When Reiki is practised our mind naturally goes into a deeply relaxed state. Therefore it is not such a huge leap to incorporate the practice of meditation with Reiki.

There are many different techniques to incorporate the two during Reiki treatments. For example, the practitioner may focus on the coming and going of the breath during the treatment or they may use visualisation and breathing techniques combined together. One such technique is that on the in breath, the practitioner imagines their body is filling with the Reiki energy and on the exhale the energy is exiting the palms of their hands and filling the area where the hands are placed with vital energy.

Before exploring the Reiki Meditations presented in this book, the following section is designed to give a deeper understanding as to how and why we meditate and how this can assist us in developing a Meditation practice that brings lasting benefit to ourselves and our Reiki abilities.

Reiki is of course flowing constantly and is not reliant upon the practitioners breathing cycle, but by meditating and giving Reiki in this way it serves to enhance the experience for all concerned.

PART TWO

ALL ABOUT MEDITATION

CHAPTER 2

WHAT IS MEDITATION?

In this section, I would like to share with you an overview of the practice of meditation and to start, it is important to identify exactly what meditation is. Because there are so many different kinds of meditations offered today from a variety of traditions and schools, it is beneficial to know what it is and how it can help us.

To begin, we should recognise that Meditation means different things to different people. The Tibetan Buddhist definition of meditation literally means "to familiarise". It is a process of becoming deeply familiar with a positive and natural state of mind.

When we meditate we subdue disturbing impressions and emotions and bring our minds under control. Like a wild horse, we can learn to tame our minds and understand ourselves better. Of course, this is no easy task as our minds are constantly moving from this to that and constantly relating to the past or the future and missing the here and now.

People often decide to learn meditation because they recognise that there is something wrong or they are dissatisfied with their current situation. Before we start we need information about how to meditate and which methods are useful. Along with this, we should also check what we are doing and not take any meditation practice on blind faith. You need to check things for yourself and be discriminating.

When looking at meditation it is important to clarify what meditation is not.

It is not about sitting cross legged, staring at ones navel and saying 'OM' every ten minutes, nor is it about falling asleep or levitating or having magical abilities. Meditation is a very direct way to know ourself and how our mind works. It brings clarity and wisdom and is something very practical and useful in daily life.

It is important also to recognise that meditation is not limited to what happens on the cushion but should be a daily living experience. In many regards what we do on the cushion in practice is a rehearsal for our life. Of course if you want to learn then at first we need to sit and practise, but with time and experience the spaces between meditation and being in the world become less and less. This does not mean that we float around on a cloud being vague or dreamy; meditation cultivates clarity, focus and awareness.

To begin the practice of meditation you need methods which work and then you need to use them. This means practise in order to gain an understanding and direct experience. The other thing is to be able to hold the level of our meditation so we don't fall back down again. This is easier to say and harder to do but with steady progression, meditation becomes less of an analytical process and more about direct experience by being in the here and now.

We can say that meditation is an activity of our mental consciousness or mind. We are very involved with the things going on in the mind such as our thoughts, emotions and the like but know little about the mind itself. So what is the mind? The mind is our consciousness. Mind is that which is recognizing the things going on and that which is aware of what is being experienced within consciousness.

The mind can be divided into sense consciousness and mental consciousness. The sense consciousness includes the experience of the senses such as smell, taste, touch, sight and hearing, whereas the mental consciousness includes the entire 'Disneyland' of experiences - our thoughts and emotions. These include our desire, anger, pride, jealousy, stupidity and ignorance. It also includes our positive emotions such as love, generosity, compassion, joy and wisdom to name a few.

Our mental consciousness also encompasses our intellectual ability as well as memories, aspirations and dreams. One way to describe the mind is like an eye. It can see everything around itself but it cannot see itself. You could also say that mind is like a clear still pond that reflects everything. It is not the things that are reflected in the still water, it is the pond itself.

My Buddhist teacher always uses the example that mind is like an ocean. The activities going on in our habitual mind are like the waves upon the ocean. We experience the waves of emotions and desires and the sea is rough and turbulent, such as when we experience our disturbing emotions. What is important is not so much the things going on in mind, such as the waves appearing on the surface of the ocean, but the ocean itself.

We can say that mind is like an ocean. It is vast and it is deep. When we meditate we have an ability to experience the depth of the ocean which is our consciousness. The more we meditate the more we become aware of the things going on in mind and can rest in this experience. Why would we do this? The reason is to bring peace and to gain distance from our habitual tendencies, thereby gaining an ability to see things as they truly are.

When we meditate we bring our mind and awareness to one place. For example, when looking under a microscope, if we move the slide we are examining, we will not be able to see anything. Likewise, when our thoughts and emotions are always in motion we cannot see things clearly. When we still our mind, it is like we are placing the slide of focus and calm into the correct place. The result is that the picture of mind's natural state is revealed, if only at first for a moment.

We can also say that mind it is not a physical thing. It has no size, colour, weight or form. Because mind is not a physical thing it is therefore not the body. Mind is also something that never dies and because it is something that never dies then following logic our mind was never born. The idea of 'just one' life, according to Buddhist Philosophy is not so. When the body dies the mind moves on from this life to another life. Mind moves from one body to the next, always experiencing as it goes. The 'ego' self on the other hand does not continue, and is experienced as the 'I'. The 'I' wrongly identifying itself to be real, forms separation: me and you; right and wrong and therefore, causes us a lot of problems. Our ego is not our mind but is constructed from our experiences from the time we are conceived, all the while believing itself to be real. The ego loves to put labels on things. For example, we look out on the street and see a car. But what makes a car, a car? When does it cease being a car? Is it a car because of our identification of it being a car, or because its nature is a car? Is it still a car if we start to dismantle it?

What if we removed the tyres, would it cease being a car? Many would answer and say 'no, it's still a car, it's just a car without any wheels'. But let us say we remove the doors and the engine and the seats and dismantle them into tiny parts. Then it may not look like much of a car, but even then we still might say it is still a car, just a car without an engine, seats, windows and doors.

What if we took the remaining shell of the car and melted it down so that it became liquefied. Would it cease to be a car at this point? When it no longer resembles a car we might at this point say 'It is no longer a car'. What if we take this further to the chemical and molecular or atomic, or even the subatomic particles which make up the metal? If we investigate this more closely we realise that there are in fact gaps between these Subatomic particles and we find space in between the subatomic particles. At which point do we consider a car to be a car or not to be a car? Without wanting to sound like 'Yoda' from 'Star Wars', the answer to this question depends on the way you look at reality.

It is a question of ones perception and identification. In truth, all phenomena is empty, but empty does not mean that we should take a nihilistic view of reality, nor does emptiness mean a big black hole and that we should get very depressed and ask ourselves the question 'what's the point in doing anything?' The point is to recognize that we have invested a tremendous amount of energy and time into a mistaken identity of reality. If we spend the same amount of time or even a small portion of that time investigating not what the eye is seeing, but recognizing the eye itself then we are closer to the truth of how things are.

The cause of most of our problems as human beings is that we take our mental experiences as being inherently lasting and real. It is our on-going hallucination and our false identification with this 'I', which is basically ignorant and which taints all of our experiences in daily life. We may catch glimpses of minds true potential in moments of being absolutely present, such as during orgasm or when we sneeze. We also might have moments of reality when faced with imminent danger, or whilst driving fast down the freeway or, similarly, being in the present moment whilst being fully engaged in a creative pursuit, like giving Reiki or during meditation. These are the moments 'in-between'. In a similar way that the gaps between the subatomic particles are space, we experience minds radiant unlimited potential in these moments. The idea of meditation is to cultivate these moments, so much so that they become our reality.

Why Meditation?

In my experience people learn to meditate for a variety of reasons. Some people want peace, some people want to learn how to understand their mind, and some people want to get enlightened. For the most part, people learn because somewhere deep inside lies dissatisfaction. Something is missing and they want to find that something.

When it comes to Reiki, people also learn Reiki for different reasons. Some learn Reiki to become proficient healers, some learn Reiki for themselves and some learn Reiki for the sole purpose of helping others. Perhaps what underlies all of these reasons, whether it be meditation, Reiki or both is that everyone is looking for happiness.

The problem is, people look for happiness in a lot of places and, a lot of the time, people look for happiness in all the wrong places. When I say 'wrong', I mean places which have no inherent and lasting source of happiness. Many people take refuge in things which are impermanent by their very nature.

We look for happiness by seeking the right relationship; the right job; the right country. We look for happiness by having all of the latest gadgets like ipods; laptops; or the latest hi-fi. It is not that by having these things that we can't enjoy them, quite often we will experience happiness by the mere fact of acquiring these things. These things do give us happiness but it is a happiness which is often short lived.

For example, when we get our new i-pod or handheld computer, or a new lounge suite, we will experience happiness but our happiness can be robbed from us so easily as soon as the item that we mistakenly took refuge in is damaged, stolen, or breaks. Also, our happiness is stolen when a newer, better, faster, or sexier looking device comes on the market.

It is the nature of our minds to continually want to improve and to grasp, all in a futile attempt to find happiness. There is nothing wrong with seeking happiness, we all do it. The question isn't really looking at the happiness, the question is what is our relationship to happiness and where do we find it? When we experience happiness from external sources the happiness is unreliable, because it is not lasting and cannot free us from our problems.

Seeking happiness in this way is a little bit like a dog chasing its own tail. Every time it turns to catch the tail, the tail moves, always out of reach. Our under-lying problem is ignorance - we simply do not see the world as it truly is.

You can look at happiness like playing a game of 'chasey' with your shadow. In this example, your shadow is happiness and you constantly chase it round and round. As long as you keep running you will never catch your shadow because it is connected to you. But when you stop, your shadow stops and you realise that it is part of you. Happiness jumps on your back and there is no separation. Happiness has found you. You become one and the same. When we meditate, we get a glimpse of this insight into our true nature.

Meditation enables us to find peace and insight into the true nature of reality by finding a place of stillness and generating positive qualities in our minds. Meditation also causes us to establish a reliable foundation upon which to understand reality.

According to the teachings of Buddhism, everything is impermanent and subject to decay. The Buddha did say however, that there is one thing which is lasting and that is recognizing ones Buddha nature.

When we meditate, we gain a deeper relationship to our true nature. Meditation is a pathway to freeing ourselves from our problems. Meditation also gives us an ability to see things in a new way. Through on-going practice we can start to see situations, people and their problems, as well as our own from a less personal perspective. Meditation gives us space to see how things are. Rather than getting involved in the dramas, we can decide to take a more active role in the comedies of life.

Meditating is a gift to our mind. It is probably one of the most important things we can do whilst we are alive. Meditation is like taking out lifetime insurance, the difference is, that it is a policy which will follow us when we die and assist us in determining where we go after we die.

When we begin to practise meditation, we may encounter our rowdy and over active habitual mind first hand. A great many people who begin to practise meditation recognize the monkey mind jumping this way and that, swinging from tree to tree, constantly seeking entertainment. This is the nature of the habitual mind. But with further practise we begin to experience glimpses of reality. As soon as we recognize a moment of peace, our habitual mind will say something like: "Oh, I'm having no thoughts" or "I'm being peaceful". You may have noticed that the recognition of a moment of peace is disrupted by our habitual mind.

Our habitual mind does this all the time. To illustrate another example, we might be walking along the street, minding our own business and experiencing a state of relative peace when we look across the street and see at a beautiful woman walking her dog.

Now we might think to ourselves… *"there is a nice looking woman. Wow, she has long hair. I must remember to go and get a haircut today. I might go to that nice hairdressing salon where that girl works who wears perfume. My auntie always wears perfume I must remember to call her for her birthday. What should I get her for her birthday? Maybe a brocade of flowers, I always get hay fever in the spring. I remember last spring when I travelled up north to see the wildflowers and couldn't stop sneezing and then the car got a flat tire. The car does need a service..."* and so our minds go along in this way.

When we meditate, we give ourselves a break from the continuous 'chat show' which is usually recalling the past or projecting into the future. Meditation enables us to experience peace and the present moment, here and now. The more we practise, the more this becomes normal and the less consistent the habitual monkey mind becomes. It's not that we don't have thoughts it is that we recognize that we are having thoughts. It's not that we don't have aspirations and desires, it's that we give up our misconceptions about them and recognize that our mistaken identity of reality is unrealistic and can't actually bring us peace. Meditation cultivates this ability to discriminate what is happening in the mind.

On an absolute level meditation enables us to cut through our disturbing emotions and to become fully self-aware or liberated. Liberation means that we are no longer the target. This means that disturbing emotions no longer have an ability to control our lives because the power which sustains them has been fully purified. We, in effect, become the master of our mind and therefore have an ability to truly benefit others in meaningful ways.

Meditation also gives us distance so that we can see what is coming up in our minds. What we do when meditating is a rehearsal of life. We gain experience and space, through meditation. When we have difficulties, meditation enables us to see things differently. Instead of responding too swiftly, we can maintain control and recognize disturbing emotions arising, which we have the choice not to act upon.

For example, you might get an email from somebody and it's not a very nice email. Naturally, you wish to defend your position and at first your ego will want to retaliate. Meditation is the ability not to press the 'send' button. It gives you space to take a moment and recognize the situation for what it is and how to respond in a meaningful way. Meditation helps us to recognize which situations to avoid and what kind of actions to cultivate. This is lasting freedom. Meditation gives such space and therefore a choice. Rather than operating out of our habitual self, we can operate from a higher perspective.

The more we meditate, we realise the things that are rising in our minds are very much like a dream. Instead of identifying with the dream as being real, we have the space to realise that it is simply things going on in mind, not the mind itself. Like waves on the surface of the ocean that come and go, by stilling our minds, the ocean becomes still and reflects its depth.

The dream of our habitual mind becomes revealed the more we meditate. This eventually enables us to wake up from the dream of ignorance. Of course not everything drops away, we still know that we are experiencing the world, but we don't identify with the ups and downs. Ups and downs simply become less personal and what is left is the true expression of our positive qualities. From this place fear subsides.

We become fearless because we are not the target and we no longer live in fear because we realise the full richness of mind. Everything that happens is an expression of mind and we naturally want to benefit others. From this place we can be a useful tool, benefiting and protecting others and showing them (through being a living example, rather than trying to change them) how they, too, can become an expression of clear awareness.

I should point out that there is a big difference between 'thinking' we're liberated and 'being' liberated. It is certainly something that does not come overnight. It takes time and effort. In this life we have built up countless negative impressions and everyone has a great deal to work through. The methods presented within this book can greatly assist you in moving through these obstacles, growing naturally and steadily.

The negative impressions in our habitual minds are like a frozen lake. If we want to go fishing in the vast waters of our true nature, we won't break through the ice of ignorance with a pickaxe if we only strike the ice once. We break through the ice by striking it in the same place over and over again. With concentrated effort, eventually we will break through. In order to achieve this, we need the right equipment. Our pickaxe needs to be sharp and strong. In other words, we need the right meditation methods. If we strike the ice here and there, nothing will happen. We need to repeat a practice over and over to have lasting benefit. If we persist we will eventually succeed.

Throughout this book I will share with you a variety of meditation practices. Some of the meditations are designed to bring the mind to a place of stillness and peace, whilst other meditations are designed to generate particular qualities and work directly with the potential of mind. Most people find the latter more entertaining. Meditation on forms of energy and light and utilising our mind and imagination gives the mind something practical to work with. Before we practise the meditations, we first need to lay a solid foundation by knowing how to meditate.

How to Meditate

It is quite beneficial when we are starting out with a regular meditation practice to do a number of things which will support our practice. The first thing we should aim for is to do the meditation practice on a regular basis.

Whether we meditate once a week for 10 minutes or daily, we should aim to do the meditation practice at roughly the same time, where possible. With regularity of practice we will establish a positive pattern in our mind.

For example, if we meditate on a Monday morning, we should try to meditate the following Monday morning, instead of finding something else to do which our ego finds more entertaining. If we are disciplined and set ourselves achievable goals, we will be more able to establish a positive pattern and in doing so, will benefit greatly with our meditation. Meditation is a real gift to yourself. It should not be seen as a chore but a blessing. Some people actually look forward to meditating.

Another factor to consider is the place where we meditate. It's best to set aside a special place for meditation, whether is it a corner of a room or a place in your house where you can be undisturbed. The place set aside for meditation should be clean and well ordered. This will have a beneficial effect on your mind, because you will associate the place with the practice. Simply being in this place will aid in training your mindset for meditation. It is also good if you can develop some kind of ritual surrounding the way you begin and end meditation. This also supports the process of meditation and is, in fact, part of the overall practice.

Whether we set our meditation cushion on the floor, light a candle, or even the way we arrange flowers all contribute to cultivating a state of mind akin to meditation. If we commence every meditation session in the same way without changing the ritual, this also supports the practice and establishes a positive pattern in our mind.

Of course, in life it is very difficult to always find peace in the outer world and inevitably, we will find ourselves in situations where we will be disturbed during our meditations.

We can see these outer disturbances, such as the neighbour mowing his lawn the moment we sit on the cushion, or children seeking our attention just as we are about to start, as disturbances or we can view these outer disturbances as opportunities to practise patience. We can choose to see all outer disturbances as a test of our ability to remain calm, focused and at peace. However, in the beginning, it is better to set aside a regular time when you won't be disturbed. You can aid this by remembering to switch off your mobile phone, take the phone off the hook and let those around you know that this is your time for meditation and that you do not wish to be disturbed.

Which Practice?

Presented in this book are a number of meditation practices. The reason for this is so that you will have a variety to choose from, as not every meditation practice in this book will be the most useful to you.

How Long to Practise

When we start meditating, it is an ideal not to set unrealistic goals such as *"today I will sit and have no thoughts for two hours"*. Rather than setting a goal like this it may be more useful to think: *"I will sit for five minutes in peace and notice my thoughts"*.

Ideally, your meditation sessions should be short, so that by the end of the session you still feel comfortable and alert in your mind. As I have said before, meditation should not be a chore but a blessing. If you are struggling with dullness and boredom, start with shorter sessions and build up gradually.

When we practise our meditation sessions it is good to be aware of what thoughts you bring to each session. It is common in life to experience ups and downs as well as good and bad days, be it from external influences or our own processes. This can all have an influence on our meditation session. It is very useful to commence a meditation session by allowing all of your thoughts and feelings to be temporarily put aside, which you can pick up again as soon as you finish the meditation session.

Most of the meditation practices presented in this book begin by a becoming aware of the breath as it comes and goes at the tip of the nose. When we focus on our breathing, this has an immediate effect on our subtle energy channels, which correspondingly affect and neutralise disturbing emotions.

Another feature of the meditations is to mentally affirm that we are now going to do a particular practice. A meditation should always begin with a clear intention. Here we place our hands in the *Gassho Mudra* (hands held in prayer position at heart level) and affirm the meditation practice which is being done.

It is also useful to be aware of your physical posture. Simply scanning the body with your awareness and being mindful of your posture at the beginning of meditation enables you to make any necessary adjustments, as well as consciously focusing our attention, to gently release and relax any areas of tension within our entire body. A full explanation on body posture will be outlined in the pages that follow.

What to Watch Out For

When you start meditation it is common that you will become overly distracted and may feel that you are not getting anywhere. Don't be too concerned by this, as it is completely normal and in time your meditations will improve. More often than not we are our own judge and jury and we are very quick to judge our meditation as being too this or that. Don't become discouraged if you are losing concentration or have disturbing emotions arise or feel agitated or overly sleepy, these are the sorts of experiences that all meditators face, without exception.

On the other hand, some people are overly confident and may think they were wonderful before they started meditating and now they are even better. When we mediate we should not put ourself above anyone else. We also should not think that the experiences we have, such as sensations, or seeing colours, is important. Nor are special abilities like levitation, reading minds, psychic powers and clairvoyance - these are possible, but they are not the ultimate goal of meditation.

Sharing Experiences

When we meditate we might have thoughts such as *"I'm the best"*; or *"I'm the worst"; "they all love me"; or "they all hate me"; or "my experience was better than his"; or "I didn't have an experience".* All of these thoughts are a complete waste of time. Recognise them for what they are - mental spam. Delete them from your inbox and carry on with the practice of meditation.

It is also advisable not to talk too much about your meditation experiences, unless you have the opportunity to speak with a meditation teacher who has years of experience to offer suitable suggestions. When we share our meditation experiences we do two things. First, we dissipate any merit associated with the experience and secondly, we give other people too many ideas and they start to compare and think they should have the same experiences. This can become discouraging for others and only leads to distraction. So like a keen poker player, one should keep one's experiences close by.

When we meditate we focus our intention inwardly. If we become overly concerned with our experiences and focus outwardly, this serves as more of a distraction than a benefit.

Meditation and Pride

With meditation we do not need to change our appearance or behaviour in order to meditate. Simply be natural. It isn't necessary to wear white flowing gowns, or become 'holier than thou' - this won't impress anybody for long.

Beware of pride. Someone who has accomplished anything with meditation generally doesn't go around telling others how great and accomplished they are. In fact, if someone does this, it is a clear indication that they are clearly not what they say they are.

An accomplished meditation practitioner has no need to advertise their accomplishments. Anyone who says that they are enlightened; is not enlightened. Be wary of people who are overly keen to tell you upon their first meeting just how accomplished they are, particularly if they are wearing flowing white gowns and come across as overly holy, this is a sure sign to be wary of such individuals.

One of the best antidotes to pride is gaining guidance under a qualified meditation master. You can learn a great deal from someone who has already mastered meditation. So finding a qualified teacher is very useful. By qualified, I mean a teacher who not only has knowledge about meditation but someone who is accomplished in meditation. A teacher must have experience, not merely information from books. A teacher must be compassionate, insightful, sincere and genuinely interested in your development, not just your purse.

If you can have confidence in the teacher and are able to communicate in a beneficial way, then this will assist you in developing at an accelerated rate. Of course you shouldn't go out on a guru expedition to find a teacher, when the time is right a good teacher will come. Your job is to recognize that time when it arrives.

CHAPTER 3

POSTURE IN SEVEN POINTS

When we meditate we may not think that posture is actually so important, but the truth of the matter is that posture plays a very important role and can directly affect the results of our meditation. Like building the foundation for a house, posture gives us every opportunity to get the most out of our meditation by cultivating a stable and firm mind. The body and mind are intimately connected, so whatever we do to the body in terms of posture will have an effect on our mind.

We can all relate to this. For example, when we feel stressed or agitated, we readily notice that our body becomes tight and our breathing may become heightened or irregular. By the same token, we know that if our body feels sluggish or tired, our mind also won't be clear.

It is well documented that the way we feel about ourselves and the way we think directly affects the experience in the body. Because one state of mind or experience of our body correspondingly affects the other, so it is true with meditation.

In Buddhism, there are seven points on posture which have been recommended by serious meditation practitioners for centuries. These points are considered by far the best way to promote positive results in meditation.

These seven points of posture refer to the legs; arms and hands; the back; the eyes; the jaw; the tongue and the head. In fact, each of these seven points corresponds to mental/emotional states and directly affects the movement of vital energy throughout the entire body.

Let us now look at each of the seven points in detail:

Legs

The first point and indeed the foundation of any posture are the legs. For many people, unless they are adept at yoga or do some kind of sport which involves flexibility and stretching, then sitting in full-lotus position, where your legs are crossed one over the other, may be considerably hard to achieve. Many people who first begin meditating in this way usually find that their knees (instead of resting somewhere comfortably on the floor) appear to be closer to their ears, so this position can be quite difficult initially. Of course, if you are unable to meditate sitting cross-legged on the floor due to past injury or age, then it is quite appropriate to sit on a chair. I will go into this option a little later.

An alternative position to full-lotus which, as I said earlier, is an advanced meditation posture even for accomplished meditation practitioners, is the half-lotus position, where the left leg is on the floor and the right foot is on top of the left or in front. See Figure 1.

Figure 1. Half Lotus sitting position.

According to the Buddhist texts, it is said that if the legs are crossed in either of these ways (half or full lotus), then this will prevent descending energy from entering the central channel of the energy body and subdues the tendency for the emotion of jealousy to arise in meditation. Now, you may be thinking that during your meditations you may not have experienced feeling overly jealous if you didn't cross your legs, but to the experienced meditation practitioner these subtle emotions have been observed when this aspect of the posture is neglected.

Of course, you can also simply sit cross-legged in whichever position is most comfortable for you. A point to remember is that when sitting on the floor there is a natural tendency for the back and shoulders to roll forward. To remedy this it is best to sit on a cushion which will tilt your pelvis forward slightly, thus enabling your shoulders to be rolled back and your spine upright.

If you are unable to sit on the floor for whatever reason, then a chair (not a lounge) or a low bench is another good alternative. One should sit on the edge of the chair so that the back is not leaning against it and with your feet planted firmly on the floor, a distance apart. This will assist in creating stability in your meditations. The most important thing is that you're comfortable and not in agony whilst sitting.

Arms and hands

Now we come to the second postural point of the arms and hands.

Here are a couple of options showing how we may hold our hands. Either with hands resting palms down, as shown in figure 2, or holding hands in the Dhyana Mudra, as shown in figure 3.

Figure 2. Half Lotus position with palms down on knees

If you choose the Dhyana Mudra, it is recommended that your hands are placed comfortably in your lap about two inches below the navel, with your right hand on top of the left and thumbs lightly touching, to form a triangle.

The right hand is on top of the left because the right hand corresponds to the activity of compassion. The left hand corresponds to the activity of wisdom and in this way the wisdom supports compassion and everything that is done on the path uses the best of both worlds.

Figure 3. The Dhyana Mudra

When your hands are in position, be aware that your shoulders are not raised and ensure your arms are relaxed. It is not recommended to hold your palms close to your body but instead move them a few inches away form your body.

When the hands are held in this position it is said that the emotions associated with anger and aversion are subdued. This aspect of the posture also prevents dullness and sleepiness, which for some people appears to be an experience which comes naturally when meditating.

Of course, there are times when you will hold your hands in a different meditation mudra, such as the meditations outlined in the section on mudras.

It is quite common, if you read other books on meditation, or observe people while meditating (particularly in new-age circles), to sit with palms facing upwards. The reason why we recommend palms down is that this represents being grounded in the present moment. It is all too easy to be drift off into sleepiness or dullness when meditating. Having the palms facing down on the knees will assist in preventing us from slipping away with the fairies.

Back

Of all the seven points of posture recommended, the back is by far the most important. Your back should be upright but relaxed. This will enable the even flow and distribution of vital energy throughout your central channel, which runs along the spine. With this point of the posture we can observe that if we are slouched forward our mind becomes dull and likewise, if we are leaning back too far, we will be distracted and become filled with pride. Leaning to the left will generate strong feelings of attachment and to the right will tend to generate feelings of anger and aggression. Sitting on an uncomfortable cushion will perhaps lead to other disturbing emotions, so choose a firm cushion which will keep your back upright and vertical yet relaxed and certainly not rigid. This will assist in promoting a sound meditation on all levels.

If you can remember to have a straight spine in your meditations, this will greatly increase the depth and clarity of your meditation practice. When we have our back straight we prevent the emotions of stupidity arising, thus I have heard from the Buddhist teachings.

Eyes

The next point of posture are the eyes. The saying goes: *"The eyes are the gateway to the Soul"* and this is certainly true, for the eyes directly connect to the energy centre in the middle of our chest, or our Heart Chakra. When we are moved or upset, the heart is moved or hurt and the result is that the eyes get wet. We also know that when we look deeply into another's eyes we genuinely meet them in a true sense.

As for how we use our eyes in meditation there is much debate amongst Reiki practitioners, teachers and the like. The debate is whether they should be closed or fully open during Reiki meditations. Here, we can say that all options are valid, depending on what kind of meditation practice you are doing and what you need to cultivate.

When a meditation requires the practitioner to simply observe their mind, whilst focusing on the breath or some outer focal point, then having the eyes open is highly recommended.

When we are doing meditations where we visualise or imagine certain things (either internally or externally) then it is recommended for the eyes to be closed. This enables the meditator to be able to focus more clearly on what is being imagined.

But having the eyes closed can bring problems associated with sleep, dreams, or dullness. It is also not recommended to do meditations lying down because before long you will find that you are no longer meditating, but fast asleep. The body has been trained for years to recognize the lying down position as a position where we rest and sleep so it is best to avoid this by sitting upright during meditation. Of course, lying down is fine to receive Reiki self-healing treatments, as we are not specifically using this as a way to meditate but rather to receive nurturing and healing from ourselves.

With regard to the emotions, the jaw, the tongue and the eyes having a slight downward gaze helps to subdue the emotion of becoming too proud.

Jaw

The next point to consider is the jaw. It is important that when we meditate the jaw is relaxed, with the teeth slightly apart and certainly not clenched. We should have an awareness that our mouth is relaxed and our lips are supple and lightly touching. We should also have an awareness of a pleasant and relaxed expression upon our face.

For some people this point of the posture can be considerably difficult, as a lot of people hold tension in their jaw or grind their teeth at night when sleeping. If you find this is your experience, then a gentle massage on your jaw from a qualified massage professional will assist in removing stress associated with this area of your body and help to reduce tension in your meditation practice.

Tongue

The next point to consider is that of the tongue. The tip of the tongue should touch the palate just behind your front teeth. The result of this is that it opens a channel or pathway of energy throughout your body and on a more practical level reduces the need to swallow constantly throughout your meditation practice, which is not only a distraction for yourself but when meditating in a group, it serves as a distraction for those around you.

Head and Neck

The last point is that of the head and neck. The head should be slightly bent forward so that your gaze is directed towards the floor in front of you, as if you were looking at something 1.5 metres in front of you.

If your head is directed towards the sky, this can lead to the mind wandering and agitation and if the head is slouched too far forward, this can lead to sleepiness.

One way I remembered the correct position of the head was from my meditation teacher. He recommended that you should think you are in a boxing ring. If your opponent took a swing at you they would miss because your chin was slightly tucked in. He always uses colourful analogies so ideas stick.

With regard to the emotions, when the head is slightly bent forward the emotions of desire and attachment are subdued.

If we can adhere to these seven points of posture, then we will keep a state of clarity in meditation. It is also advisable to assist in promoting and supporting these points of meditation, so that if you have the opportunity to learn some form of physical exercise such as Yoga or Pilates, this will encourage a more comfortable experience when meditating.

At the end of the day however, if you are experiencing more pain than pleasure in your meditation, then opt for a more comfortable posture such as sitting in a chair, so that meditation is not a chore but a gift to yourself.

CHAPTER 4

THE FOUR CONTEMPLATIONS

The four contemplations, which turn our attention to why we should meditate, come to us from the Tibetan Buddhist tradition. Although Reiki is not Buddhism per say, these four teachings are beneficial no matter what kind of meditation we choose to do. These contemplations are very important because they help us to make choices about the lives we lead.

These four thoughts include:

The precious human life;
The impermanent nature of all existence;
The contemplations on cause and effect or 'Karma';
The contemplations on the results of cause and effect or understanding the conditioned world.

Before you commence meditation, I encourage you to take a few moments to contemplate the following four teachings and see how they fit with your life. You should think about these four contemplations and see if they have meaning for you. You need to know these teachings on a personal and experiential level for them to have any lasting meaning and benefit.

The Precious Human Life

The first contemplation is to recognize our precious opportunity in this life to know our minds through spiritual teachings. What that means is that we should try to make as many good choices in order to live a meaningful life.

When we are young, we tend to focus on things which are not so important such as wearing the right clothes, having the right jewellery, talking the right way and generally maintaining a heightened state of 'Cool'. The problem is, what is cool today, may not be what it is cool tomorrow. It is also not enough to only be focused on whether our football team will win or what is happening on reality TV, we need to use our time now to work intelligently and develop spiritually. This first contemplation is there for us to recognize that we have a real opportunity in this life to wake up.

We should also recognize just how lucky we truly are. If you have the ability to purchase this book then you are already doing considerably better than the majority of people on the planet. A great many people do not even know where the next meal will come from, let alone have an opportunity to encounter practices and teachings which will enable them to develop their minds in a meaningful and lasting way. It is pretty hard to think about liberation and cultivating our true potential if we are caught in the experience of basic survival. We can also be thankful that we have not been born in a third world country, which is gripped by famine and war.

If we look at the law of cause and effect, (which is the third contemplation), we can say that the reason why we have these opportunities is because of previous conditions coming into being. You could thank your previous incarnations for doing a great deal of good. Without your former 'selves', what you are experiencing right now in your life would not be possible. On the other hand, for any difficulties that you are experiencing right now you can also thank your previous selves, because everything that we experience in our life is due to cause and effect. Of course, if you don't believe in past lives this is quite okay, but in your next life you probably will!

The contemplation of the precious human life also extends to recognizing that we have all of the sensory facilities in tact which enable us to learn, understand and develop. This includes the senses of sight, hearing, touch, smell and taste. It also includes the mental capacity to learn and understand. If we are mentally retarded for example, we are disadvantaged compared to somebody with an average IQ level. This is not to say that somebody with a mental disability cannot benefit, but there is an obvious disadvantage.

Of course, there are many people in the world today who simply have no sense for spiritual things. Whether they are struggling for survival in difficult circumstances where there is no possibility for spiritual teachings, or whether they live in the world of the rich and famous without a care in the world, there is neither chance nor apparent need to look deeper.

When one has everything one could ever need it can be easy to be distracted by this and not spare a thought for spiritual practice. This is not to say that we need to be poor or live an aesthetic lifestyle, the point is to recognize that whether we are living in a war zone or in the glitz and glamour of 'Hollywood', the opportunity to practise meditation (for the most part) eludes such people.

Another point about the precious human life is having a correct understanding of things. This means not being confused and seeing something which is good as bad and likewise seeing something bad as being something good. It is considered fortunate to be able to recognize the truth in situations, which is not always easy to achieve. When we look at our precious opportunity, it is about having an attitude of gratitude and not taking things for granted. The teaching on the precious human life is about cultivating a real motivation for life. Not to waste our time in senseless pursuits or destroy or confuse our body and mind with drugs or other abusive additions. It is about using our time well and to benefit others.

The first contemplation ultimately motivates us to practise meditation, without being either nihilistic or existential, but seeing the unlimited potential we all have here and now to recognize our true nature.

Impermanence

One thing that we can readily observe in our lives is that impermanence is everywhere. Nothing is fixed or lasting. Ageing seems to be the only way to live a long life but with age, we also notice that our face changes and our youthful appearance which we treasure, begins to give way to decline. Gradually, we obtain new lines and the things that used to defy gravity no longer defy gravity. So, our physical body is always changing and no matter what we do to try and hold on, the changes come. No amount of youth cream or cosmetics can prevent the inevitable progression of ageing, despite what the advertisements want you to believe.

We also know impermanence with our emotions. These too are constantly changing.

One minute we feel happy and the next minute we feel sad. Emotions come and go. We are up and then down constantly in our lives. Many of us have experienced just how quickly our emotions can change. One moment a friend will say or do something and the love that we felt is suddenly consumed by anger and frustration. Emotions can change so quickly.

We can also say that our thoughts are continually changing. This is perhaps one of the most common experiences. Because our thoughts are always darting from here to there like a monkey swinging from branch to branch, so it is with our thoughts and emotions.

When it comes to health we also know that it is inevitable that if we feel well, that eventually at some point, we will feel unwell. We never think about illness when we are well but when it comes, all we think about are the symptoms of our illness and cling to the hope of a return to wellness.

Another certainty is death, a subject we try to avoid. The problem is everybody dies. As the great Buddhist master Nagarjuna said *"There are many things that can harm our life, for it is impermanent like a bubble on water that can burst by the wind. It is a great miracle that after exhaling we take our next breath, and after falling asleep, we wake up again."*

Although we don't like to think about it, our inevitable demise will come one day. The only question is where and when? One thing that is uncertain is when death will come because death does not follow any rules. We know this to be true because children do not necessarily live longer than their parents and teachers do not necessarily die before their students. This is one of the problems with being alive. We do not know when death will come.

When we die we always die alone, no matter how close our family and friends are. It is something we cannot do with another, the journey is solo. Even our shadow, which has been with us our entire life cannot come with us when we die. There is nowhere we can go to escape it. We could not hide in a secluded forest or upon a high mountain. There is nowhere where we can go or hide to escape death. It always has an uncanny ability to find us.

We can also see impermanence exists with all sense objects. The new car will eventually break down and our new white shirt will receive a new stain. All our possessions will be stolen or lost and our new technology will be superseded by new technology. All things change, decay or die.

We also cannot rely on our relationships. Even the person we love and hold dear will eventually die or leave. Our love may leave us for the other person, or the love that we cherish and hold dear may become stale.

We also cannot rely entirely on our family. Even if we have a close loving relationship, families split up, move away, pass away or are separated through unfortunate circumstances.

We also cannot rely on our job because this can also change. We might be replaced by someone who is younger and more talented, or our company may go into bankruptcy or we may have an accident and no longer be able to work.

Our health will also most certainly change. We will get sick, injured or too old to work.

As you read this, the idea is not to let these words get you down and depressed, it is to recognise how things are. The contemplation on impermanence is not so that you will feel pessimistic and begin to give up thinking *"I am going to die and therefore there is nothing I can do"*, this is not the point of the contemplation.

The whole point of meditating upon impermanence is to inspire us to practise meditation. We cannot rely on our friends or possessions or some God in the sky. It is completely up to us what will happen. All that we do know sows the seeds for our future. The point is to give up our negative actions and to stop planting bad seeds and instead do what we can now to make a better future for ourselves.

The only thing we can rely on is cultivating the true nature of our mind. It's not going to matter how much money we have, or how many possessions or friends, or how much we are admired. When we die, none of this matters. What does matter is what positive impressions we have generated in our mind. This is where meditation comes in.

Impermanence is designed to inspire us to practise meditation and to set aside wrong views and harmful actions. By cultivating positive actions and working diligently towards cultivating a true nature we grow something which will help us in this life, when we die and in our future lives. It enables us to live better, die better and be reborn better.

Cause and effect or 'Karma'

The central idea of cause and effect or Karma is that positive actions lead to positive results and negative actions lead to negative results.

For cause and effect to leave the deepest imprints on our minds, there needs to be four ingredients:

The first of these is to know how a situation is; the second is the wish to do something; the third is to do the thing or have it done; and the fourth is to be satisfied at the end.

If you are missing some of these four elements, then the power associated with cause and effect will not be as strong.

This makes more sense when we illustrate cause and effect with a strong example such as killing. In this example, the first condition suggests that we need to know how the situation is, which means we know this is a human being who has the capacity to experience suffering. The second condition is that we decide to kill this person. The third condition is the actual killing, whether we carry this out ourselves or arrange someone to do the 'job' for us. The fourth condition is that we are satisfied with the outcome. This brings about the strongest effect, and will leave a very strong imprint upon our mind. However, there are different degrees of cause and effect.

Using the same example of killing, we could imagine we are driving down the road on a dark and rainy night. The visibility is poor and suddenly we hear a 'thump-thump' and we know something has happened.

Fearing the worst, we stop the car and to our horror, we discover that we have assisted another being in completing their life. Now, it is not that we set out that day thinking "tonight I am going to run over a pedestrian" but the fact is, a being has met unexpectedly with our vehicle. The result was that the life was taken, but we feel remorseful.

So, in this for example, only two of the four ingredients came together. We participated in the end, taking the life of another, but we did not set out to do this. We knew it was a human being we killed, but we felt terrible afterwards. In cases like this, the results of cause and effect are certainly not as strong as in the first example.

On a more positive note, as it turns out, our story has a happy ending. A few minutes later, another car stops and low and behold, the driver is an off duty ambulance worker. It just so happens that he has all of the emergency equipment with him and tends to the unfortunate person. He soon realises that the person is not dead but simply knocked unconscious. Despite a few broken bones and some internal injuries, with the care of the off-duty ambulance worker, our pedestrian lives to walk another stormy evening in the rain. We could say that this too is cause and effect in action, because the pedestrian had the good fortune to have the assistance of something that could help.

When you look at cause and effect, essentially there are three points:

The first point has to do with the building up of causes and conditions which become our future. Then there is a second point, which has to do with living through the results of causes and conditions and what comes out of these. The third point has to do with how we get out of cause and effect by transforming it.

On the level of our body, cause and effect also plays a part. It determines what kind of body we get, whether it is a healthy body or an unhealthy body and what kind of genes we received from our parents.

Then there are the results of what kind of situation we find ourselves in. Cause and effect determines whether we are born into a country which is peaceful or a country which is in war. For example, we might be born in deepest, darkest Africa, or we might be born in a Western country with freedoms and opportunities. Cause and effect determines whether we have opportunities to be educated and to develop in a meaningful way, or whether we are in a situation of survival and have no real opportunity to even consider a spiritual path. If we're wondering where our next meal is coming from, then we probably don't have much time to sit down and meditate, let alone have the opportunity to meet with teachings that can enable us to develop in this way.

Cause and effect also determines the kind of tendencies we have. Whether we naturally want to harm or help others.

Most people live their lives by holding onto what they like - pushing away what they don't like - keeping what they have found and arranging themselves according to whatever they cannot change.

In order to go beyond cause and effect, the first thing we need to recognise is that something is wrong. The second thing is that we need to want to do something about it. The third thing is to decide not to do harmful things again and the fourth thing is to seek to do the opposite.

Some common misunderstandings about cause and effect

The first thing one should know is that cause and effect is not something like fate or divine retribution. Whatever hasn't happened yet can be changed. There is no one doing something to us, making things happen, it is all the result of our previous actions. It is up to us what will happen. All of our former thoughts, words and actions have become our current situation and likewise everything that we say do and think will be sowing the seeds for our future.

There isn't the idea in Buddhism that there is some kind of God, which is directing our lives. Everything we experience is the result of our own actions. This idea is extremely liberating because we have the opportunity to be entirely responsible for our lives and situations. Instead of pointing the finger outside ourselves, we can recognize that the cactuses we are sitting in right now, we put there. Understanding karma gives us a choice. We can get up, pull the spikes from our behind and get on with doing something beneficial. We have an opportunity to be self-reliant and responsible people. This frees us because it gives us a choice. No longer being a victim of fate, we can actively participate in meaningful situations, knowing that we will be benefiting ourselves here and now, as well as in the future.

Another wrong view about cause and effect is that results appear straight away. As John Lennon's famous lyrics state *"Instant karma's gonna get you"* Most people think that cause and effect is played out very directly, but this is not the case. For example, we get angry at our neighbour and the next moment we trip over the step and hurt ourselves. But this is not how cause and effect works. It takes time for impressions to ripen. Just like a farmer who plants seeds, a crop will not appear right away. When we do something, be it positive or negative, it takes time for the results to manifest.

The other thing to recognise that there is no such thing as shared karma. We may think this is true when we look at ants on an ant hill, but this is not so. All beings have their own karma. Sometimes beings with a similar karma come together in one time and place, so it will appear that there is a shared karma or collective experience. Each being has their mind and therefore their own karma.

Cause and effect is also happening all the time both outwardly and inwardly. For example, if you fill milk into a car instead of petrol you will get a certain result. On an inner level if we generate positive impressions we will get that positive feedback. Many spiritual traditions understand that whatever exists on the outer level must surely exist on the inner level. It cannot operate only outwardly as to say otherwise does not follow logic.

Other misconceptions about cause and effect include the idea of losing free will. Some people argue that if everything is cause and effect free will is lost. But free will is the knowing that we have an ability to shape our present and future circumstances. Cause and effect means that *we* are the creator of our experiences. Not an outer creator, or other people, or other circumstances.

Some people have the misconception that cause and effect only applies to people who believe in it. The fact is that cause and effect is a universal law that applies to all beings, whether they know it or believe in it. Once we realise that we are sowing the seeds for our future, we can make a conscious choice to give up harmful and negative actions and practise generosity and kindness wherever we can.

The Flaws of Conditioned Existence
The fourth contemplation has to do with the results of the third contemplation, cause and effect. With the fourth contemplation, we consider the faults of conditioned existence. By contemplating the disadvantages of physical existence, we turn our attention away from it which enables us to be less concerned with outer things and to turn our attention to more meaningful experiences.

Part of the classical contemplations from Buddhism is to first consider that no matter in which realm of existence beings exist, there is always suffering. As human beings, we experience old-age, sickness and death, but all other realms of existence also experience suffering.

There is much suffering concerned with being human. There is the pain and misery that comes along with daily life, but there is also pain and suffering because of the things that we are attached to. As soon as there is change involved from losing something we once had, we suffer.

This final contemplation motivates us to cut through our longing for outer circumstances and instead joyfully strive to realise the true potential of our mind through the practice of meditation. It is only by practising meditation that we can move forward in a speedy fashion towards liberation and perfect enlightenment.

As human beings there are fundamentally three types of suffering:
• the suffering of change;
• the suffering of suffering; and
• the suffering of everything composite

The first of these is the suffering of change. At some point in our lives we may feel satisfied and complete and as soon as circumstances change we suffer, due to our strong attachment. An example might be having a delicious meal. We enjoy all of the fine foods and the exquisite taste only to realise sometime later that we have eaten too much. We might also have had some physical reaction to the food and then we feel terribly sick.

Another example: we may be purchasing a new car. On our first day, we drive it to the supermarket. We go shopping and come back only to discover that somebody has hit the back of our brand new car. We suffer because the thing that we invested our happiness in has suddenly changed.

The second kind of suffering is the actual suffering of suffering. What this means is that we may be having some kind of difficulty, and then before that suffering is complete, a new suffering commences. An example of this happened when I was travelling through Peru. As many travellers will relate to, I had the good fortune of getting dysentery. Just as I thought to myself that things were bad, the very next meal I had resulted in food poisoning. On top of that, because I felt quite rundown and exhausted from all the travel, I also came down with a fever. It was one thing after the next. There was a great deal of the suffering of suffering. We have all probably experienced similar things. Just when you think it couldn't get any worse, something else happens.

The third kind of suffering is the suffering of everything composite. We can be going through our life and at times experiencing happiness. We might think to ourselves that everything actually seems pretty fine. The fact is, because of our very situation, suffering is everywhere. We need only look to the evening news or to pick up a newspaper and we will see that there is endless suffering all around. The majority of things that go on in this world are done through greed and selfish actions. By simply buying a product from the supermarket we may be inadvertently participating in an unwholesome activity, because the product may have been produced through great hardship. For example, you might buy coffee beans where the workers were exploited. This is the world we live in and for the most part, it is simply unavoidable.

But what of our human condition? Here, there are additional phases of suffering. These are the suffering of birth, old age, sickness and death.

Many people have a romantic idea about a baby in a mother's womb, but being born is not all that it's cracked up to be. We have suffering the moment consciousness enters into the womb of our mother. Aside from cramped conditions, when the mother eats hot food, the unborn baby experiences pain and suffering and likewise, when the mother eats or drinks something cold, the baby experiences the suffering of coldness.

If the mother eats too much, this brings with it a feeling of being squashed. When the mother walks, the motion is like being bounced up and down in the wind. When the pregnancy reaches full term, there is of course great suffering experienced by being born. Aside from the suffering and pain experienced by the mother, the baby experiences being squeezed through a very narrow opening, which is both difficult and painful.

Once the baby is born, they are pretty much helpless and reliant on the kindness of those around them. Leave a newborn unattended for a short time after birth with no care and they will die. So being born is a very vulnerable place to be in. A newborn cannot communicate what it wants. It has to deal with the suffering of hunger and the embarrassment of soiling itself endlessly. For the most part, we can readily observe that a newborn baby suffers and cries a great deal. Of course it's not all bad - babies also experience happiness and joy. The point is, suffering is never far away and is an inevitable part of life.

Then there is the suffering of old-age. When we're young, healthy and full of energy, we don't think much of old-age. But provided we reach old age, the experience of the suffering of old-age will soon be upon us. When we are old, our body becomes weak and loses its energy. Eating certain foods becomes difficult and even our taste buds diminish. Our mental faculties also weaken. We lapse into confusion and forgetfulness. Our teeth fall out and eventually we can no longer choose solid food.

Eventually, our body loses heat and we become very weak and are no longer able to carry anything heavy. We find that even the most simple of tasks become impossible. Our joints and fingers become riddled with pain and our legs and arms become arthritic. We find it very difficult to stand or sit, our flesh becomes old and wrinkled, with blemishes. As the years pass our youthful appearance slips away in front of the mirror.

If you have ever had the opportunity to visit an old people's home, you will see the physical and mental experiences of old-age first-hand. Of course, we don't want to look too closely at such places. For the most part, they are unpleasant to observe but for the serious meditator. Visiting a home for the old is a direct way of experiencing the contemplation of old-age.

Then there is of course the suffering of sickness, which comes in any manner of forms. No matter how vital, radiant, and healthy we may seem, sooner or later sickness will find us. We know from practising Reiki that we have an ability to help ourselves but even then, there are times when we experience illness regardless of what we do.

To experience sickness directly, we only need to visit our local hospital or the reception waiting room at the nearest doctor's surgery. Of course, for people who are experiencing very serious illnesses such as cancer or multiple sclerosis, the suffering of such illnesses are long and painful.

When we are sick this makes us short tempered and unable to turn our minds towards positive things, because the discomfort that is caused by the disease pervades our mind. We can't do the things we like to do and we are no help to anyone, least of all ourselves.

Then there is the suffering of death. When death comes, there is very little we can do. We no longer have the strength to get up and move around. Our body becomes completely weak and we have anxiety and a foreboding feeling of what awaits us.

If you are lucky you have family and friends gathered around you, but there is nothing they can do to delay your inevitable departure. There is also nothing we can take with us on our journey. Our favourite friend or any of our possessions, they are all left behind. We may also experience remorse of the things that we have done, but by then it is too late. Death comes and just like one who has not made any preparations for a long journey ahead, suddenly we are faced with an unknown future.

When people are interviewed and asked what is the thing they fear the most, death as well as public speaking rate highest. Although public speaking is nowhere near as terrifying (in my opinion) as death, some would venture to differ in this opinion.

In our lives we experience suffering which can take many forms. It includes the fear of meeting with people who do not like us, the fear of losing the ones that we love and then there is the suffering that comes from not getting what we want. We also suffer when we encounter the things that we do not want. Even if we live a wholesome and positive life, we will experience jealousy from others and there will always be somebody who wants to take what we have achieved.

If we become wealthy and acquire luxurious possessions, then it is often the case that we would need to guard those things to protect them from being stolen.

Because there are people who seek to gain our wealth, we worry and invest a tremendous amount of energy in protecting these things. No matter what we do there will be those who do not cherish us. There will be those who dislike us and this also causes us suffering.

Then we fear losing our loved ones. When those loved ones leave, whether it is through a new relationship or we are separated through hardships or through death we will suffer and experience a great deal of anguish. This is the suffering of separation.

Then there is the suffering of not getting what you want. We may strive for certain situations to achieve certain goals. For whatever reason, we do not achieve what it is that we set out to achieve, something gets in the way. Especially when we have invested a lot of energy into these hopes and aspirations and they do not come to fruition, again, we experience suffering because we have not achieved what it is that we wanted to achieve. This can lead to an experience of depression and hopelessness because all of the opportunities and possibilities of our life have passed us by.

When we encounter things that we do not want we also suffer. Suddenly certain situations manifest and we have to deal with those things as best we can. If we are attached to what we want and what we don't want (which is part of the human condition), then we will always have difficulties.

All this talk of suffering is not designed to fill us with a sense of depression and dread but rather is a contemplation to motivate us, they are much like the previous contemplations designed to motivate us to use our time well and to actively do things which benefit ourselves and all other beings.

When contemplating these four thoughts before we meditate, it enables us to bring the right kind of attitude to our meditation.

We recognize that by coming to understand our present situation and to know that there is something seriously wrong, that we will actively do something beneficial to understand our minds. It is only by coming to understand our true nature that we can truly be of lasting benefit to both ourselves and others.

It is for this reason that these four contemplations are presented. If we enter into our meditation with the wrong view and intention, although we may develop on some level, development will be more stable and more lasting by approaching a meditation with a correct understanding of how things are. The four contemplations give us this understanding and motivation. Once we have contemplated the four thoughts, we move onto the next stages of meditation.

In order to gain an overview of meditation as a whole, the following is an explanation of the common stages of meditation.

CHAPTER 5

THE STAGES OF MEDITATION

Most of the meditations presented in this book can be divided into five stages. These are:

* establishing posture;
* establishing intention;
* the body of the meditation;
* the dissolving phase; and
* the sharing of merit.

We will now look at each of these five stages.

Establishing Posture

Before we begin the meditation, we should prepare the space for meditation. This includes setting up our meditation chair or cushion and making sure that family members, including pets, are not going to disturb our session. We should remember to switch off our mobile phone and set our telephone to the silent mode, or simply unplug it from the socket.

Once we have set up the space around us, we establish a sound posture for meditation.

Attending to the seven points of posture* (which include: the legs; arms and hands; the back; the eyes; the jaw; the tongue; and the head), we prepare ourselves both mentally and physically for the meditation to follow.

{* see previous section on the seven points of posture.}

Establishing Intention

The second stage is to establish our intention. When we commence a meditation, it is important to state which meditation we wish to commence. Establishing intention also means to cultivate the right motivation for doing the meditation practice.

The four contemplations just explained are an excellent way to cultivate the right motivation. When we meditate, we should do it for the right reasons and that is to benefit others. These four thoughts motivate us to meditate. It is beneficial to think about these and ask the question *"why do I want to meditate and what to I hope to gain from meditating?"* The stronger we can make our motivation for the practice, the more benefit we will achieve by doing it. Most importantly, we should think that we not only do our meditation practice purely for our own sake, but for the benefit of all existence.

When we come from a place that shares the good with others, it helps us to cultivate a richness of mind. Through the process of direct identification, where we *"act like a Buddha until we become a Buddha"*, as we think, so (eventually) we become.

In Buddhism, this is known as cultivating *bodhichitta,* which translates to generating the mind for enlightenment. *Bodhichitta* includes the aspiration to become an enlightened being in order to help others, with the upmost love and compassion. It might be hard at first to genuinely experience this feeling of love and compassion for all beings, therefore it is sometimes easier to begin with those we are close to, us such as our family, friends, loved ones, children and even our pets.

Once we have cultivated this *bodhichitta* mind, it becomes easier to extend this feeling of love and compassion to those 'tough customers' we encounter in life. This, in itself, is a meditation practice.

Whichever way we choose to generate our intention and motivation, this should be done before we commence our meditation session, as this sets the scene for what will follow.

Just in the same way as taking a journey to a place we've never been, establishing a sound motivation is like checking the roadmap and coming to an understanding of how to achieve that destination in the most care-free, simple and beneficial manner.

The Body of the Meditation

Once we have established our intention, we calm our mind by becoming aware of the coming and going of the breath at the tip of our nose and we let all thoughts and feelings just go by.

Watching the breath helps us to hold the mind in one place. Once we have stilled the mind, we then bring something beneficial out from this place. We also balance and harmonise the inner and outer energies in the body through the awareness of the breath.

From this place, the body of the meditation commences. In the third phase, we spend the most time and hopefully, achieve the greatest rewards. Whether we are meditating on a particular mudra, or engaging in a meditation which involves imagining energy and light, we should always be mindful that we are present and when we notice that our mind has 'left the building', we bring ourselves back time and time again, to the practice at hand.

What isn't useful is to think: "Oh no, I've lost it again" but rather just simply bring the mind back to the object of the meditation and carry on.

When thoughts come and go, it is like being in a busy railway station. We observe the trains coming into the station and stopping. We see people getting on board and then we see the trains leaving. Attending to our meditation is like noticing the trains coming and going, rather than hopping on and going on a journey. If, or perhaps I should say 'when', we notice that we have jumped on a train (which, incidentally, is a train of thought – pun intended), we should bring ourselves back to the station of peace and mindfulness and continue on with the practice.

Depending on the meditation practice that you are doing, this may also involve a building up phase, where we generate forms of energy and light out of space, or imagine channels of energy throughout our body. This additional phase of activity is where we interact with forms of energy and light, according to the particular practice. Whenever we do meditations of this kind, is it important to dissolve these visualizations, which I will explain in the following section.

The Dissolving Phase

Many meditations presented in this book have a dissolving phase. What this means is that whatever is imagined or produced in mind is put away back into mind. It is not common that we will leave what we have generated in the practice out in space.

We can think of the dissolving phase as like packing away our luggage after having been on a long journey. When we leave our hotel, we don't leave all our things lying around, we pack them away neat and tidy and take our bag with us. It is like putting a signature at the end of a letter and remembering to write a full stop at the end of a sentence.

When we engage in a dissolving phase, we mix everything that we have generated in mind back into ourselves. In this way, we recognize that it is not something which is permanent or fixed, nor is it something which resides outside ourselves, but something which has sprung forth from our unlimited potential and in this way is self-empowering and cultivates self-reliance.

Sharing of Merit

Every time we complete a meditation, we generate some positive energy. Despite the perceived results of our meditation, some good has occurred simply by doing it. The reason for this is that meditation is a non-ordinary activity and by simply engaging in meditation we will generate positive energies within our body and our environment.

If you have something which is good then why not share it? When we dedicate the merit, we actively think that whatever peace of mind, happiness and joy has been generated by doing the meditation, be shared not only for our benefit, but for the benefit of all lives.

We may choose to make this dedication in a general sense, or, if there is someone we know who could really benefit, or someone who is in need, we can think that all the merit that has been generated from this practice be now shared with the person concerned.

When sharing the merit for another, we make the wish that they may regain their health, or that they may receive some positive energy as a result of the meditation. Sharing the merit is a little bit like making wishes for others. When sharing this intention, it also empowers our life energy. We do it because we realise that we are just one and there are many.

Sharing the merit also generates a feeling of generosity and a sense of sharing. As a result, we start to see the world in an unlimited fashion, abundant and full of potential.

CHAPTER 6

THE GAPS BETWEEN MEDITATION

We should think of meditation not as an isolated incident in our day, but a rehearsal for the play of our life. You could say that meditation is not just what happens when sitting on the cushion but more importantly, it is taking the experience of peace out into the world. Therefore, it isn't necessary to draw distinctions between before and after the meditation, but instead to see all things as an extension of meditation.

This does not mean that we should be walking around in some kind of dream. What it does mean is that we see the possibilities and potential in the world around us. We can think that all people that we encounter have the potential for happiness.

When we see others suffering, we can recognize this as mind's ability to be disturbed and when we see others experience happiness, we can see this as mind's ability to experience joy. It is about cultivating a pure view of reality. It is about seeing the highest good in all people and in all situations.

In today's world, we can clearly see that there appears to be a lot more dramas than there are comedies. It is very easy to get caught up in negativity and by the problems of those around us, as well as our own. The secret is that if you focus on problems, you only strengthen them. If you focus on that which is good, you give power to that.

Meditation affords us the opportunity to see the world through a new lens. Not just rose tinted glasses, but seeing the world through the eyes of love, compassion and wisdom.

Ideally, we should try to avoid being a 'Sunday Meditator'. What I mean by this is to try not to be the person who only meditates once in a while. Therefore, regular practice is most important.

Our life is a meditation. We can commence with the first thought that we have upon waking. It is an interesting exercise to be aware of your first thought. For some people the first thought is *"oh no, not again"*, or *"I need more sleep"*, or *"I have to go to work"*, or other things which I shouldn't write in this book.

Our first thought sets the tone of our day. Just in the same way that setting our intention at the beginning of a meditation sets the scene for the actual practice, so it is that our first thought sets the scene for our day to unfold.

One way to begin your day is to make wishes. Establish a sound intention for the kind of day you wish to have. Similarly, when you go to sleep, you should give thanks for the things that you experienced that day. You can review what you understood or gained throughout your day. It is good to bring with this a sense of gratitude in your heart and think that whatever good has been generated, be shared with all that lives.

When we experience any challenge or difficulty, we can see it as a purification and as something that has now left us. We should also wish for whatever or whoever was difficult, everything that is good as well. This sets the scene for a restful sleep.

The goal of daily meditation is to experience the whole of our lives as meditation. No separation between outer, inner, object and action. We recognize all of these things as being parts of the same unlimited totality. That is, the unlimited potential and free play of our minds.

The Conditions for Practising Meditation

In this section, we will discuss the right conditions for practising meditation.

These teachings are traditionally taught in Tibetan Buddhism and are designed to support the practice of meditation in a very practical sense. The following points outline the conditions that we need for practising meditation, including the obstacles which can arise during meditation and the remedies to these obstacles.

When we meditate it is beneficial to be aware of both the outer and inner conditions which support meditation practice. This includes finding an appropriate place to meditate where we will not be disturbed by outer influences. In addition to this, we also need to cultivate the right intention, such as not being too obsessed with our desires and thinking about the things we want. Nor is it beneficial to place overly high expectations upon ourselves.

We should also be happy with our current situation. If we are constantly striving for things in the outer world, this will creep into our meditation and we will not be able to be focused in any serious fashion. The idea is to be able to put our desires 'on hold' for a time, so that we can be sincere with what we are doing in meditation.

If we are too busy in our lives, involved with this and that, we will have a great deal of difficulty in our meditation, that is, if we can find the time in the first place.

When we are too busy, we will find our mind is constantly preoccupied by these outer things. It can be very difficult to slow down and to benefit from our meditation and therefore, it has a great deal to do with our attitude.

When it comes to being able to hold the level of our meditation, we can support this by having good conduct. What this means is avoiding negative actions which bring harm to others. This advice might seem like common sense, but it is so easy to slip into negative actions, words and thoughts.

The reason for this advice is that if we have negative actions prior to meditating, even in the same day, the energy of that negative action will be close to us and can easily disturb our meditation practice. This, of course, is good advice to follow anyway in life, whether we meditate or not, but it is especially important if we intend to have beneficial results from practising meditation.

CHAPTER 7

OBSTACLES TO PRACTISING MEDITATION

Very often when people start meditating, they notice that they become the worst kind of people. All of the things they have suppressed and kept under the surface begin to rear their ugly heads. It is when we are still that we more readily notice the ups and downs, and those things which distress us. Of course, many people are distressed and disturbed anyway and when they become aware of these disturbances, they often blame meditation as the cause and stop practising. This is an erroneous view, because the practice of meditation is simply showing them what needs to be purified.

The good news is that what is experienced in mind is not you, it is a by-product of disturbing emotions and stiff ideas which are changeable. When we meditate, we have an opportunity to recognize a certain level of detachment. These disturbing emotions can actively be transformed by applying the following antidotes to the obstacles that can arise in meditation.

When we meditate, there are eight different kinds of obstacles, or disturbing states of mind which can prevent us from meditating properly. These include agitation; regret; heaviness; dullness; doubt; wishing harm; attachment; and drowsiness.

Let us now examine each of these disturbances and their antidotes in greater detail.

The first obstacle: Agitation

The first and most common disturbance is agitation. Here, we experience our body and mind as being overly active and either wanting more, or disliking something or someone.

When we worry about outer things, we are certainly not meditating. When we think about such things we feel agitated. When we are agitated, we will also notice this in our posture. For example, our eyes will look around the room and our hands will feel restless. We may even notice how our head wants to rise upwards. These are all clear signs that agitation is in full swing. We can also be distracted by outer things like sounds. Whether pleasant or unpleasant, agitation can arise and take us away from our meditation.

It is quite often in life that we are unaware of our minds and simply let agitation roam freely. It can be quite challenging to slow down an agitated and restless mind.

The remedy for Agitation

The way to overcome agitation is to contemplate the impermanent nature of reality. If we are constantly agitated because we are worrying about the future or the past, it does not benefit ourselves or anybody else. Everything is constantly in motion and everything we experience in our lives are but moments in time. When we recognize that nothing is permanent, we realise the futility of investing an agitatied mind into things.

Another way we can change our state of agitation is to contemplate old age, sickness and death. Knowing we will die someday, the idea of getting uptight really seems like a complete waste of time and energy.

When we meditate, a practical thing to do when we feel overly agitated is to imagine a black ball of light coming down, into and through the top of our head. The black ball then slowly descends through the central energy and comes to a resting place at the base of our body. The attention on this ball falling through our body has a calming and restful affect. Once we feel more restful, we can move our attention back to the practice at hand.

Another alternative is to restate your intention for meditating. With this intention strengthened, your determination will increase and the agitation is subdued. Agitation can also be a sign that your posture needs correcting. If your head has moved and your spine is not straight, this can lead to your mind becoming more restless.

Allowing the eyes to rest comfortably 1.5 metres in front of you with your chin slightly tucked in and your spine straight, will immediately have a beneficial effect. If agitation continues throughout the meditation and you simply cannot settle, you may need to discharge excessive energy. This can be achieved through physical exercise, or a brisk walk. It is also important to remind yourself that achieving deeper states of meditation takes time and patience, so don't be too hard on yourself when you are starting out.

The second obstacle: Regret

Sometimes when we are meditating, we might think about something that we regret and although it has already passed and cannot be changed, nevertheless, we still feel regret arising in our minds.

The remedy for Regret

When the feeling of regret arises in our minds, it is important to realise that regret is about something which is in the past and cannot be changed - the only thing we can change is our relationship to the things we regret. If we are still feeling remorseful and sorry for the harmful things we have done, we can, of course, apologise to those concerned. This enables us to move on. But when regret arises in meditation, we should try to let it go. The simple acknowledgement of the thought of regret is often enough.

We may think: *"I acknowledge this feeling of regret arising in my mind. I will now put it aside and continue with my meditation."*

Once acknowledged, we can re-direct our awareness to the meditation at hand instead of getting into the memories and situations surrounding the past situation which caused the emotion in the first place.

The third obstacle: Heaviness

Experiencing heaviness has to do with previous causes and conditions ripening in one's life. When we want to do something beneficial like meditating, we find that we feel heavy and likewise, when we feel heaviness, we will want to do something which isn't so beneficial.

The remedy for Heaviness

When we experience heaviness in meditation, the best way to overcome it is to generate confidence in our teachers and spiritual ideals. If we can think of teachers that inspire us, such as great spiritual leaders, this inspiration will bring us out of heaviness and instil confidence in our meditation.

The fourth obstacle: Dullness

Dullness or a lack of clarity is different to the feeling of heaviness. Both heaviness and dullness are connected to previous causes and conditions, but dullness is strongly linked to our health and physical state. If we feel dullness, it can have to do with a lack of physical health or exercise or even our diet.

The remedy for Dullness

When we experience dullness in meditation, it is best to generate the feeling of encouragement. This means feeling that by doing a meditation we will see positive results, rather than being hard on ourselves. We should encourage ourselves by thinking that we are benefiting ourselves and others by doing meditation practice. Here, encouragement is the key.

We may also take note of which foods make us feel dull and heavy and which foods leave us feeling light and aware. Avoiding certain foods which promote heaviness may help to overcome dullness in meditation as does regular exercise.

The fifth obstacle: Doubt

This is when you start to doubt whether doing the meditation practice is going to be of any benefit. You may think to yourself: *"Who knows if this is really going to work for me and maybe there's something else I could do that would be faster and more effective than doing this meditation"*. If we have thoughts like this, we will not meditate very well, because the doubt is constantly taking us from our meditation and slows down our progress.

The remedy for Doubt

When doubt arises during meditation, the remedy is not to give it any energy whatsoever. It is best to simply continue on with the practice. Another way to overcome the feeling of doubt is to look at meditation in a logical way. We can do this by examining our doubt, to see if it really has some basis. Then we can look at the benefits of meditation by thinking about how other people have benefited. If we simply abandon it, we will only generate more of the same problems we have now.

In this way, we can logically come to understand that doubt has no benefit and will not lead us anywhere meaningful. We also need to be realistic. The majority of our life has been dedicated to avoiding the true nature of our minds. This hasn't helped us till now, so maybe we should continue, to see if this practice helps.

We should also not be too hard on ourselves if we did not turn into a rainbow after the first meditation session. The results of meditation and practice come gradually.

Always do your best to be patient with yourself. There is nothing to be gained by thinking that it is the meditation which is the cause of your new-found problems. The fact is that if you want to turn a rough diamond into a radiant one, you polish it. Polishing it once will not reveal its radiance. You need to polish it again and again and again. So it is with meditation. The more you practise, the more you will be filled with positive impressions. Eventually, there is no separation and you will become full, radiant and pure like a polished diamond.

The sixth obstacle: Wishing harm

We may experience, during our meditation, our mind wandering off in different directions and we may start to think about people who we dislike or who dislike us. We see everything that is wrong about them and we experience feelings of jealously or anger, or we think that we are so much better than them. When such thoughts and feelings arise, pride and arrogance has stepped into our meditation. These are all expressions of wishing harm.

When we experience these disturbances, it is all too easy to see the faults of others but it is very hard to see our own problems. Like a finger which is pointing outside, we tend not to focus on the fingers pointing back to our self.

The remedy for wishing harm

When we wish others harm, we are clearly not operating out of a place of compassion.

We keep planting the seeds for misfortune again and again. As soon as we have taken a position of ourself being right and others being wrong, our pride is running the emotional rollercoaster. When we recognise we have placed ourself above another, we should kick out the pedestal which we have created for ourselves and come down to the level of those around us. When we experience pride, we are always in bad company, because nobody can be at our level and this can be quite a lonely place.

There is, of course, a useful kind of pride and this is the inclusive kind, where we think how great we all are together. By cultivating a strong sense of solidarity and seeing the potential of a group of like-minded people, there comes a place where we can really make things happen for the benefit of all concerned.

So, the way to remedy ill-will is to do exactly the opposite. Here, we generate and contemplate kindness towards the ones we wish harm. It is easiest to generate kindness when we think of our friends and family, but it is much harder to cultivate the same feelings for difficult customers. To do this, we first think about those we love, then call to mind those we feel indifferent to, then extend these feelings to the ones we have challenges with.

We can also look at wishing harm to others by taking things less personal. When we see that wishing harm to others only increases our own troubles, we soon recognize the futility of such thoughts and feelings. Seeing things from the other's perspective is also a beneficial way to not get caught up in these thoughts and feelings.

When we contemplate and meditate on loving kindness, we also benefit the environment around us. We start to generate a positive energy field in our place of practice and anyone who visits this place also benefits. You have probably had the experience of walking into a room where someone has been meditating, or a place where people frequently conduct positive activities such as healing and nurturing positive development. The experience is peaceful and pleasant. Visiting a temple or a holy place will also cultivate this positive feeling. This is where the positive life energy of the place rubs off on you and you benefit from the merit and activities from others' practise.

The seventh obstacle: Attachment

This is where we have many desires. We have desires to possess a person, a status or desires for things that please our senses. For example, we may have a strong feeling that we 'need' potato chips or some other food which takes our fancy. Strong feelings of attachment can be a big distraction during meditation.

The remedy for Attachment

When we have attachment, it takes a lot of our attention and energy, so the best remedy for attachment is contentment. We should focus upon what we have right now and generate a feeling of contentment. When we have contentment in the 'here and now', we stop focussing on what we do not or can not have. Focusing on what we cannot have only brings more problems. The emotion of attachment is vast, so in chapter 9 there will be a more in-depth commentary on how to overcome it.

The eighth obstacle: Drowsiness

This can be a common experience for people who meditate. If you observe a person meditating and you notice that their head has fallen forward and their eyes are staring somewhere in the direction of their navel, this is a clear indication that the drowsiness has won. Snoring sounds are also another dead giveaway, so drowsiness can be seen very readily in one's meditation posture.

The remedy for Drowsiness

If we feel drowsy in meditation, it can be that we simply have not had enough rest. One way to overcome drowsiness is to meditate on a soft clear red light. We imagine this red light rising up through our body and out through the top of our head. Of course, if a lack of sleep is truly the reason, then it might be more useful to take a break from meditating and go to sleep instead. Once you are fresh and have revitalised yourself, then you can once again sit down and meditate with better results.

A splash of cold water on your face can also help to subdue drowsiness. When drowsiness features strongly in meditation, some additional suggestions include meditating with your eyes wide open, or it may also be helpful to have more light in the room where you are practising.

CHAPTER 8

OVERCOMING OTHER OBSTACLES

In addition to the eight obstacles just mentioned, there are many other mundane distractions which a practitioner may encounter. These obstacles include disturbances from outer sounds and noise; physical discomforts; physical sensations and imagery. The following is an explanation of these and how to deal with them.

Outer disturbances of sound and noise

No matter where we are, we will encounter sounds and noise, whether perceived as being pleasant or unpleasant. We may be living in a busy city, where the sounds of traffic and the noisy neighbours disturb our meditation, or we may be meditating and experience pleasant sounds such as birds tweeting, or the sound of the wind through the trees. Both kinds of sounds can be a trigger to distract ourselves from meditation. Either pleasant or unpleasant can be a problem. It all depends on our relationship to sound.

We could say it isn't the sound that is the problem, it is how we relate to it. If we like a sound will we will feel attraction and if we dislike a sound we will feel aversion.

Aversion and attraction are both obstacles in meditation. When we hear a sound, we start to identify with it and have memories about similar sounds or associations with those sounds. For example, we may hear the sound of a ticking clock and think about a ticking bomb or the sound of a dripping tap and think about doing the dishes. Our minds make judgements about sounds, which can lead to agitation and therefore less meditation.

One of the best ways to deal with sound is to name them. For example, you could be meditating and hear the sound of a motorbike riding past your house. Rather than getting into an extended fantasy about the motorbike or the rider, simply state the word 'motorbike' then return to our meditation.

By naming the sound we can move on, as naming has an ability to cut through.

Of course, it is useful to find a place to meditate which is not so noisy (although all sounds are mantras and expressions of wisdom) when we are beginning, it might be hard to recognize this. Try to choose a place and time when sounds are less likely to disturb you.

If you find that you are being plagued by excessive noise, then think of it as an opportunity to practise patience. You may think to yourself: *"Now I have a real opportunity to see how well I can meditate with all of these outer disturbances, the universe must be giving me an opportunity to test my abilities."*

Physical discomforts and the body

I once saw a sign on somebody's desk, which said: *"Don't ask me to relax it is only the stress which is holding me together!"* In our modern society, I think that many of us can relate to this. When first beginning to meditate, one of the most common themes experienced is physical discomfort. Many people are so used to operating in stressful ways that by the time they slow down, the body finally has a chance to point to the areas which need relaxation.

In an extreme sense, when the body is overly stressed and not given an opportunity to relax, stress can manifest in the form of diseases such as cancers and the like.

If you find that your discomforts are many when meditating, then there are a number of beneficial exercises you can do. The first is to mentally scan your body. Start at the head and move systematically down through your body, all the way to the fingers and toes. As you scan through your body, isolate your awareness in specific areas. You can then make a mental note of which areas hold the most discomfort. Once you have isolated these areas, you can imagine that you are breathing energy into these areas. As you inhale, imagine that these areas are being filled with radiant energy. As you exhale, imagine all of the stress and tension is dissolving, like ice blocks in a cup of hot water. With each breath more and more of the pain and tension leaves your body.

Another way to deal with physical discomfort is to imagine that the areas where you hold tension dissolve into emptiness. Instead of tight muscles in your back, imagine that these dissolve and become radiant space. You can extend this practice throughout your entire body until there is only a thin membrane of light holding your physical form together. This short exercise can be very beneficial for releasing stress and discomfort throughout the body.

On a very practical level, if you are experiencing physical discomfort due to your meditation posture, it is quite alright to adjust or change your position so that you are more comfortable or simply take a break and stretch your legs. Walk around the room and then sit down again and continue. The idea of *'no pain, no gain'* does not apply to meditation practice.

Overcoming physical sensations and imagery

When we meditate, aside from feeling physical discomforts, we can also experience a variety of sensations and subtle experiences such as tingling; lightness; a sense of the body expanding or shrinking; a feeling that your awareness is leaving your body or that all parts of your body dissolve and fade away. If you experience any of these sensations, the idea is not to be overly concerned nor engaged in these experiences.

Although these experiences are pleasant and interesting, we should not pay too much attention to them, nor try to repeat them. A good meditator is attached to neither bliss nor discomfort.

In the same way that you would notice an unpleasant sensation arising, so it is that we should simply observe or notice whatever feelings or sensations arise and not give them any attention. In due course these sensations will naturally subside.

It is also common to experience pictures or images in the mind. This includes seeing colours behind our eyes or images appearing before us or in our imagination. Again, we should not pay too much attention to these transitory experiences, simply acknowledge them and again they should naturally subside.

More often than not, these are impressions which are being processed through the sub-conscious mind. They are much like the pictures which arise in our dreams. We encounter this 'natural filtering' of impressions during meditation. All of these experiences are reactions to being in a non-ordinary state of consciousness, which is meditation. The trick is to make meditation an ordinary experience.

If you continually experience more extreme sensations and pictures on a regular basis, then it may be advisable to seek the guidance of a qualified meditation teacher, or seek the necessary therapy to assist you in gaining a deeper insight into these experiences. However, for the most part, experiences such as these are simply 'Disneyland' for the mind.

Changes that comes through Meditation

When we start meditating, we can often become increasingly more sensitive, both through our senses and on an emotional level. We also experience things more intuitively. It is not uncommon to experience a spacious quality of mind where we will know who's ringing on the phone before we pick it up, or we may think about a person and the next day we receive their e-mail or run into them in the street.

We may also notice that our senses are heightened, so that colours seem more brilliant and vivid and our sense of smell and touch also become heightened.

We may become more sensitive to substances that are more 'dense' in vibration. For example, we may notice our tolerance to alcohol decreases, as it does for unhealthy foods and non-purified water. In particular, we may become aware of the people around us.

In the past, we may have noticed that certain individuals who were difficult affected us, but we could nevertheless tolerate them. But once we begin meditating, we become overly sensitive to other people's disturbing tendencies. The fact is that we may not have noticed them being disturbing but now that we are meditating it becomes more apparent, due to our heightened sensitivity.

This may cause some concern and we may question how beneficial all of this meditation stuff really is but the fact is, we are simply becoming more attuned to our senses and emotions and this is a natural by-product of meditation.

Naturally, when we experience that we are being disturbed by others, it usually has very little to do with them and everything to do with our view. But because of our habitual tendencies, we think they are the ones who need changing. In most cases, it is profoundly stupid to try and change others. If you have ever tried this, you will see that it is a fruitless exercise. The fact is, there is no one we can change - all we can do is set a fine example. By this, I do not mean that we should be presenting ourselves as someone holy and righteous but rather, we should set a positive example by simply being who we are and generating a positive mind. It is through our actions and our positive attitude that we set an example for others to follow. Any change will come by others seeing how you have changed for the better and they may become inspired to do the same.

When we change, others notice and they are usually the first to notice. They may begin to question: *"why are you so nice these days?"* or *"you never seem to be in a bad mood, what are you doing that's different?"* The philosophy of Reiki and meditation is to become a living example of the teachings, as there is nothing to be gained by becoming a 'Reiki missionary'.

CHAPTER 9

OVERCOMING DISTURBING EMOTIONS

Recognizing that we cannot change others and that the only thing we can change is our mind is the most useful place to start. The more we meditate, the more we purify our disturbing emotions. As a result, we may notice that feelings such as anger or irritation as well as attachment or desire, depression and fear may arise.

It is important to know how to deal with these disturbing emotions. The first thing we should know is that although the disturbing emotions are disturbing, we should accept that having these emotions is perfectly normal and human. We should not think that we are spiritually inferior in any way nor should we think that we are a bad or evil person for having them.

One way to overcome disturbing emotions is simply not to take them seriously. It is also good to see if they have any real value. One thing we can do is to ask others if they are interested in purchasing your disturbing emotions. We might ask them how much they will give us for our anger, for example. You can even advertise it in such a way that it is going really cheap but what you will find is that nobody is interested in buying your anger. You can therefore conclude that your anger has no real value.

What do we do if we have something which has no value, do we keep it and cherish it or do we throw it away? Realising that it has no lasting value, the answer is to throw it away. Like a computer program which causes our computer to crash, the program of disturbing emotions only causes problems for our mind. There is no point is keeping them as they benefit no one.

Another way to deal with disturbing emotions is to simply change our view. Instead of getting upset when we didn't get what we wanted, we can tell ourselves that what has happened is exactly what we wanted. For example, we might have to speak to somebody from the telephone company who is not offering the best service. Instead of getting upset, and seeing this situation as being 'wrong' we can think to ourselves that this is really a great opportunity to learn patience. Alternatively, we can look at the situation compassionately and think what it must be like for the person at the other end. Maybe this is their 50th call today and the customer service representative is probably tired and stressed out. We can think that this person could really use our kindness, understanding and support. We should never hesitate to offer kindness, not even for a second. Have you ever noticed how well things flow with kindness?

According to the Buddha's teachings there are 84,000 different combinations of disturbing emotions. I have not counted them, but the most common include anger, attachment, jealousy, fear and depression. The following is a detailed examination of each one with a variety of suggestions for transforming them.

Dealing with Anger

Disturbing emotions, like everything else in life, come and go and are therefore impermanent by nature. For example, we might have a feeling of anger as a result of a conversation or experience with a loved one. How long we choose to experience the emotion of anger is entirely up to ourselves. Anger is an emotion which cannot last for a very long time without our continual focus upon it.

We know this to be true because after we have had an argument and all is forgiven, there is no anger to be found. It is also interesting to point out that anger is not just a fiery experience of rage, it also can be classified by any subtle experience of aversion or dislike.

Disturbing emotions come and go in your mind but the emotions are *not* your mind but are happening '*in*' your mind. Think about it like watching a movie. The pictures come and go on the screen of our mind but the screen is simply a surface for the pictures to be seen.

When dealing with anger, we should neither express nor suppress the emotion. Both methods are destructive. If we experience anger and suppress it, especially over a long period of time, we will create great disturbances in our mind and body. It has long been recognized that if we are calm and relaxed, our physical body will function efficiently. Anger and, in particular, suppressed anger can lead to stomach ulcers and other physical diseases. If we express anger, we can also cause a great deal of disturbing impressions in our mind and in the minds of others. What is useful is an honest acknowledgement of the emotion and then implementing a variety of techniques to gain detachment and understanding and thereby, transforming it.

When we look at anger there are essentially two kinds - cold and hot anger. Cold anger is the type that says *"I will get you later"*. This kind of anger slowly smoulders and is like the embers of a fire. This kind of anger can smoulder for very long periods of time. All it needs is to be fed little by little to be sustained. Conversely, hot anger comes in a way that cannot be sustained for extended periods. This is like the strong emotion of rage. It takes a tremendous amount of power and energy. We can observe this when we see somebody getting angry and they become very red in the face, which can escalate to become explosive anger. The angry person begins to look quite unpleasant and can be experienced as being completely without control. When someone is 'hot' angry, they lack all clarity and control in their mind and do not see things clearly. For example, in boxing or other competitive sports, a common tactic is to get the opponent or the other team angry. If you succeed, you will surely win because when your opponent operates out of anger, their skill and decision-making abilities decrease tremendously.

When people are angry, they often feel justified in expressing their anger. They think that by expressing their anger they will get their way, or teach the other a lesson. In most cases this only leads to further problems or embarrassing situations which they will regret later on.

On the other hand, when people suppress anger it is often because they do not feel strong enough to stand up and say what they truly feel. Not expressing anger does not mean that one 'turns the other cheek' - what it means is that we act with strength and intelligence.

By knowing our mind, we have an ability to discriminate and benefit ourselves and others in meaningful ways.

This is not to say that you become your own therapist, as many of our habitual emotions are heavily ingrained. If, by implementing the various techniques described in this book, you still require assistance with your problems, then it is quite alright to seek the guidance and support of a caring therapist. Meditation alone is not necessarily the solution to all our problems. We should therefore use discernment and our commonsense.

One way to deal with anger is to look at the results. When we are angry, our thinking becomes confused and irrational. Our face becomes disfigured and red and our mind becomes disturbed and fragmented. When we are angry, we generally find ourselves in embarrassing situations. We do, say and think stupid things which we only regret later. We can save ourselves a great deal of embarrassment by giving anger no voice.

The other thing is to consider is how anger affects those around us. As the saying goes *"we always hurt the ones we love"*. This is so true of anger. An outburst of anger can really hurt those around us. There isn't a great deal of wisdom in hurting the ones we love. Anger also leaves strong negative impressions on our minds. Any positive merit that we have accumulated through meditation can be destroyed through an outburst of anger. This makes anger very expensive from a spiritual perspective. We simply cannot afford to destroy our positive merit that comes through spiritual practice.

Giving anger a voice is like voting for a dictator. If we put it into power then the real trouble will start. Anger is also a real obstacle to cultivating love and compassion. It hinders our progress on the spiritual path. When we recognize the harmful results of anger, we realise that it is an associate we cannot afford to keep.

Another point to consider is cause and effect associated with anger. When we get angry it is often because we don't get the things that we want, or it is because we lose the things that we have. When these things happen in life, it is useful to remember cause and effect. Everything that we experience (pleasant or unpleasant) is due to previous causes and conditions ripening. We were the ones creating those conditions. When we experience negative things, it is an opportunity for us to be patient, rather than retaliating and pointing the finger somewhere else.

Realising cause and effect and what we do right now is sowing the seeds for our future, another method is to think about what your future self will experience from your anger. Do you think your future self would thank you or resent you for what you are currently sowing? It bears thinking about.

Another method which is a common suggestion of modern psychology is to imagine yourself in the other person's shoes. In this way we can take things less personally and secondly, we can start to see what is making this person behave the way they do.

We experience anger because we want to defend our belief or point of view and the last thing we usually consider is the other person's perspective. By stepping into their shoes we gain their perspective and therefore, gain an insight into their behaviour and why they are responding the way they are. This takes the emphasis off ourself and, in this way, we know how better to respond.

When we have very difficult customers, then compassion might be the thought:

"they have to spend 24 hours a day with themselves and I only see them for one hour, it must be hard for them to be with themselves all the time". This can be one way to start cultivating compassion.

Another way is to find at least one good quality in that person. Even if this means that they have really nice taste in clothes. It could be difficult at first to find a positive quality in their personality, so a beginning point is to find a good quality about what they have or what they do. For example, this person may really 'press your buttons' but they are very good in business and they have nice friends. When anger is strong, this can be a way to approach generating greater understanding.

Another way to overcome anger is to give the person the anger is directed to, a really nice gift. The gift giving is not to say that they will see how wonderful you are, the motivation is to practice generosity. It will come as such a surprise that it will be difficult for them to maintain their anger.

Of course we should give a gift which is beneficial, useful and meaningful and not give them a gift which would cause them despair. It is also appropriate to think *"by giving this gift may I defuse whatever harm and tension that lies between us"*, as opposed to buying a gift that will teach them a lesson about how nice you are when they are so horrible. This is not the right way to view it.

I received this teaching on anger from my Buddhist master. At the time, he was giving many discourses on disturbing emotions and was using skilful teachings in very direct ways. As a result, he rubbed up against a few of his close students' egos, which caused them all kinds of inner turmoil. At the end of the lecture, he gave a teaching on gift giving as a means to remove anger and cultivate a generous heart of love. The following day sitting upon his table were several gifts given to him by the same students. The Master said simply *"It appears the teachings are sinking in".*

When others are acting in an angry and disturbed way and directing this to us, rather than take it personally, we should reflect upon our own experiences of being angry. We can gain an insight into what they may be experiencing. In this way, we no longer are the target of their anger and can use wisdom to see a higher view. This is where we can see the other person who is in anger as someone who is suffering and therefore, in need of our compassion. We are less likely to react with this understanding and instead, regard them with love and compassion, for this is surely what they need.

But what about the people we meet who we instantly take a dislike to? We should first examine our own faults. It is easy to see the faults in another, but it is hard to see our own. Therefore, examine what it is that you do not like in the person and see if this dislike relates to an aspect where you have trouble. These are called our 'blind spots'.

When you take a moment to contemplate this, you might suddenly realise that you share the same bad habit you see in the other person. When we recognise this, we will see the other person in a new light.

It is also the case that there are times when we take a dislike to somebody due to previous karma. It is not uncommon that great enemies over time become great friends. When we experience great attraction or great aversion this is an indication of previous causes and conditions manifesting here and now. We should always take notice when this happens because this is an indication that we can gain something truly beneficial from the situation.

It is also important to recognize that anger can arise in our minds when we ourselves are feeling depressed or disconnected. If we are feeling irritated (even about small things), it is best to sit down, meditate and look at what's going on in the greater parts of your life.

If you're feeling dissatisfied about something, then you can start to be more critical of what is going on and then take positive action to change the situation. It is, of course, up to you what will happen. No one else can do that for you.

When a situation is very difficult, you many find it hard to navigate through your emotions and it is quite a good idea to gain the help and expertise of an understanding and qualified counsellor or therapist. It is always good to recognize that there are things that are positive about yourself and your life. In this way, we have no need to operate from the perspective of anger.

Another way to deal with anger is to identify with who is angry. Here, we meditate on the empty nature of reality. To be angry we first need to find an 'I'. One technique is to repeat *"who is angry?"* Each time we ask the question 'who is angry?' our mind will have a reply. We ask the question again and again and continue asking the question until the power behind the emotion dissipates. This form of self enquiry can be applied to any disturbing emotion and forms an alternative way to view reality. In essence, everything is empty, but this view can be quite difficult to achieve as beginners.

When we see the world as a dream, we realised that emotions come and go and have no real substance. We know this to be true because one minute we can be angry and the next minute the anger is gone. The following day we can experience happiness and, likewise, moments later the happiness goes. Dreams are also like this, yet appear to be real. When we see the world as a dream on an absolute level, we recognise that the dramas are also not real.

Another contemplation to defuse anger is to think about death. Imagine you just had an argument with a loved one. You got in your car and because of your anger you blindly drive off. You do not see the red light or the truck coming your way. Imagine if you died today. How important would your quarrel be?

The Buddha said: *"You too will die someday, knowing this, how can you quarrel?"*

If we can live our lives as if it was our last, there would be no room for anger or other disturbing emotions. When dying patients are interviewed they rarely say: *"I wish I could get revenge on this or that person"*, what they do say is that they wished they had a chance for more time with their friends and loved ones and families. Knowing this we should use what time we have left in a meaningful and beneficial way.

We should also remember that when we get angry, we tend to do stupid things. When anger arises it is not a good solution to go out and do something physical, such as washing the dishes. When anger is on the rise, we will most likely break the dishes, cut our hand and create a mess. Only when you know anger has peaked and is subsiding should you put the residual energy of anger to work.

If we do need to release the energy associated with anger, then it is best to release this energy upon something non-sentient like a stone, or chopping wood. A brisk walk is also useful, provided you remember to look left and right when crossing the street.

At the highest level, the way to deal with anger is simply to allow the thief to come to an empty house. What this means is we do not give anger any energy whatsoever. We simply notice that it arises in our minds, it plays around in space and by giving it nothing, it eventually subsides. The thief cannot steal our happiness.

By holding this highest view, anger can be purified. By moving through your life with a deep feeling of gratitude and practising generosity, as well as actively benefiting others, the emotion of anger can have no foundation in our body or mind. This does not mean that we become sentimental or soft instead, we use the true freedom and fearlessness of active compassion, generosity and wisdom throughout our lives.

The more we can generate a positive view and see things from the highest level, the less personal things seem. We become a useful tool for benefiting others. By thinking about what we do like and becoming excited and interested in this, we have less of a chance to focus on what we do not like. Therefore, keeping a pure view is the highest way to deal with anger or any disturbing emotion.

Dealing with Attachment

Attachment is essentially a false assumption that whatever it is that we want will bring us happiness. Attachment is to want something and not be separated from that. Of course this causes problems because, naturally, life will cause separations and as a result, we will suffer because of the thing which has been lost.

Of all the disturbing emotions, attachment is perhaps one of the more difficult ones to find fault with, because we so strongly identify with attachment as being something which brings us happiness and deep satisfaction. The problem with attachment (also known as desire) is that it simply breeds more of the same because we are working on the false assumption that the thing that we want is the cause of our happiness. Therefore, we want more of it and this leads to more desire and the cycle continues.

Attachment takes many forms. People are attached to other people, relation-ships and substances such as drugs and alcohol. Most people would argue that attachment to substances such as drugs and alcohol is not such a good idea, but when it comes to relationships many people wonder what is wrong with being attached to another.

The problem is people confuse love and attachment. Love is something which is all-encompassing and unselfish in attitude, whereas attachment is concerned with our own desires and needs and is essentially a selfish attitude.

The first thing we should recognize is that having strong attachment does not enable us to have a clear and peaceful state of mind. With constant desire we are not at peace, because we are always striving and clinging to something which does not fill our desire. When we are then separated from the object (which we think will make us happy), we experience the pain of separation and spend a great deal of time and energy projecting fantasies surrounding the thing that we were attached too.

Because of this false assumption that attachment gives us happiness, it prevents us from recognizing what is meaningful here and now. One way to overcome attachment is to contemplate that all things are impermanent. What we desire is changing and will not last. Even if it is our life partner or the cherished love affair, inevitably things will change. Recognizing this, we can change our relationship to it. This is not to say that we give up on the relationship and neglect to express our love, it is to recognize that attachment is something which can create suffering simply by its nature.

Another way is to imagine that the person that we are strongly attracted to is now 50 years older. We can imagine them as old and wrinkled, hunched over and frail. *"Where is the beauty of the body now"*, we may ask ourselves? Of course, we do not do this exercise so that we will feel repulsed and have an aversion to the person we are attracted to, the aim is to exaggerate our perception and thereby change our relationship to the attachment.

Dealing with Jealousy

Jealousy is one of those sticky emotions which seems to need very little energy to be sustained. It can linger on and on for weeks. In my experience, the best way to deal with jealousy is to wish as much as we can for the thing that we are jealous of.

For example, if we are jealous of our partner getting attention from others, we simply imagine they are getting even more, so much so that we can no longer take our emotion seriously. We imagine that instead of one lover, the entire football team is making our girl friend very happy.

Do whatever you can to make the emotion of jealousy seem ridiculous and wish them everything we are jealous of. In this way, all of the energy we have invested in the emotion of jealousy will lose its power and no longer take our happiness hostage.

Dealing with Fear

Fear can be described with the following acronym.

F = false
E = energy
A = appearing
R= real

We tend to fear what we do not understand or know. If we have fear, whether it is a phobia or an irrational fear about something, this can cause us a great deal of negativity and also disturbs our peace of mind.

The way people usually deal with their fears is by not dealing with them. They either avoid situations that make them feel fearful, or run away from situations when they suddenly encounter them. The more they try to suppress their fears and ignore or deny them, the more the fear grows and becomes ingrained in the mind.

The thing we should aim to do is to gain a relationship to the thing that we fear. In doing so, we gain an understanding of what is behind the fear and thereby change our attitude towards it.

One way to deal with fear is simply to allow yourself to be in a calm space and then call to mind or imagine you are the observer and that you are seeing yourself in a fearful situation. Just like watching a movie, but the character in the movie is yourself. Imagine you are sitting in the movie theatre watching the movie of yourself in the fearful situation.

As you watch yourself in this way, begin to analyse the situation and think about why you are fearful. For example, perhaps your fear is of speaking in public and you see yourself in the worst possible scenario. Then think to yourself whether you have a chance to change the outcome. Of course, if we cannot change the situation and our worst fear is realised, then what is the point in investing so much energy and worry about it?

We can simply be patient and accept the consequences as they fall. However, for the most part our fears are irrational and have no basis in the outer world.

By gaining a relationship to the things which cause fear, we understand the fear and ourselves better. It becomes a practice of embracing that which we fear.

Another way to prepare yourself when going into a potentially fearful situation is to generate a positive motivation that whatever happens, you will be able to benefit those concerned. If the fear concerns others, we wish them everything good. By placing the emphasis on the others, it takes away the identification with a 'me' that fears.

It is important to mention that there is also a useful element of fear. Fear enables us to look left and right when we cross the road. This is the fear that keeps us alive and motivates us to look after our life. We ought to be able to recognize dangerous situations and to take necessary action to remove ourself or another from harm's way.

Dealing with Depression

When it comes to dealing with depression, we first need to consider that there are essentially two different kinds. The first is short-term depression, which is due to a particular problem or illness and the second kind is long-term depression which is caused by genetic or biological factors and may be better suited to a therapeutic environment or even medical intervention.

The following methods are beneficial for short-term depression.

When someone is in depression, they are totally focused on their problem and have invested a tremendous amount of time and energy into building up this problem. Because they are in this state of mind, they tend to attract additional experiences to reinforce this belief or experience and frequently encounter those who will re-affirm this belief in their problems.

Depressed people attract other unhappy and depressed people. It is the law of 'like attracts like'. If we are depressed and are constantly putting out the feeling of depression, the universe correspondingly gives us an answer. For those of us who are feeling sorry for ourselves knowingly, then this is considered to be quite a stupid thing to do, because we are simply not seeing things how they are. Of course, everybody makes mistakes and we don't always have control over how things will turn out, but when a problem arises, we always have a choice about how we deal with it. It doesn't benefit ourself or anybody else by sinking deeper into our unhappiness.

The best way to deal with depression is to analyse what benefit comes from depression. We can begin by determining what it is that we are depressed about. By putting this into some definitive statement we can know our foe. For example, it might be *"nobody loves me"* or *"I am hopeless in relationships"* or whatever it might be. When we analyse this deeper we tend to see that this is not actually so. The truth of the matter is although we may not be fantastic at a particular thing, there are many things that we are good at.

Focusing on what it is that we are good at and do have, can be an excellent way to overcome depression. When we focus upon what it is that we have and what we are grateful for it is very difficult to feel sorry for ourselves for too long.

Another way to deal with depression is to recognize that all mental activity, whether it is happiness or depression are all expressions of mental energy, which is non-physical and constantly in motion. If our mental activity has no form, why give it all that physical attention? This is where we meditate on the impermanent nature of our emotions.

We can think to ourselves: *"I wasn't depressed last week, but now something bad happens and I'm feeling depressed, but this too will change because it is unlikely that I will be depressed a week from now."* If we are experiencing a low, it's quite okay to be in that, but the choice is always to make a definitive change to move out of depression and into something meaningful, simply by deciding to do so.

Another way to deal with depression is to consider the suffering of other beings. When we look at all of the negative and unhappy experiences as well as the tremendous suffering that is experienced by people other than ourselves, we realise that our unhappiness is nothing by comparison.

Finally, one last way to take the emphasis off self is to go out and actively help others. We may choose to do some volunteer work, or to do some physical exercise or join a club. You might participate in a group where people are expressing their creativity. Then you'll actively meet new people, which will bring new light into your life.

If we are stuck in a rut, sometimes the best thing we can do is create a change and go beyond our self-limiting views and embrace a grander and more positive view of reality.

PART THREE

MEDITATION PRACTICES

CHAPTER 10

THE MEDITATIONS AND PRACTICES

Now that we have laid a foundation for the practice of meditation, this next section goes into a variety of practical 'hands-on' meditations, utilising a variety of methods to suit your needs. My recommendation is to try each of the following meditations presented in your own time, giving yourself a chance to experience these 'first hand'. Once you have had a chance to practise a little, you will soon get a feeling for which of these practices attract and suit you best.

The following meditations are designed to cultivate mental calm and awareness.

Meditations for Relaxation and Cultivating Awareness

The meditations which follow are relatively simple meditations which will enable your mind to find a peaceful place, to calmly abide with awareness. Not wanting anything, nor ignoring or pushing anything away. To simply rest in the true radiant awareness and unlimited potential of our minds.

It is important to recognize that Meditation is not an escape nor is it a time to go to asleep. Meditation is a way to rehearse a state of mind which is entirely natural and gives us space to see things as they are.

By cultivating awareness through meditation, we are more adept to handle the ups and downs of life without taking things too personally. The following meditation, entitled 'closed fist, open fist' is a way to attain deep relaxation by experiencing the extremes of tension and relaxation as well as transforming disturbing emotions.

Closed Fist, Open Fist Meditation

This Meditation is an excellent practice for transforming disturbing emotions. Closed Fist, Open Fist, as the name suggests, is a two phase meditation where we first summon any lesser emotions into our closed fists. The second phase is where we release the emotions and experience the opposite feeling. Whether we are feeling stressed out or just emotional, this meditation only takes a couple of minutes and can be done anywhere.

The Closed Fist, Open Fist Meditation

Sit comfortably in a place where you will not be disturbed for a few minutes. Close your eyes and take a few deep breaths. Now, feel into your body. Imagine you are able to see where you are holding tension, stress or disturbing emotions and where these reside within your body. You might imagine these lesser energies as black blotches of energy or as black smoke.

On your next in breath*, clench both your fists, holding them as tight as you can. As soon as your fists are clenched, imagine that all of the black blotches of energy or black smoke, representing the lesser energies, are immediately drawn to your fists.

As you hold these energies in your fists, Reiki energy also begins to build up in your hands. This radiant, clear light now increases more and more and all of the lesser energies and tensions dissolve.

On your out breath, slowly release your fists and begin to gradually open your hands. Relax your body and rest your palms on your thighs, with the palms up. Now imagine that all of the lesser energies have been completely dissolved by the clear light emanating from your palms. This light continues to radiate and fill the space above and around your palms.

Repeat the process as many times as you like, or until you feel a change.

Once you feel you have released tension, continue to breathe slowly and gently, enjoying the sensation that everything harmful and disturbing has now been cleansed.

* Note: During the in breath and out breath, we clench and release our fists, but it is okay to breathe normally in between, in order to imagine the phases of the meditation.

Skin, Flesh, Bones Meditation

Skin, Flesh, Bones is a meditation from the Zen tradition. It has been adapted slightly here and is a meditation on the body. Through three phases we focus on our skin, followed by our internal organs and flesh, followed by our skeletal system. One meditation aid for this practice is to look at an anatomy book, where one will find illustrations of the human body presented in the various layers. This can be useful in strengthening what we imagine during this practice.

Skin, Flesh, Bones is a meditation which is beneficial because it assists us in gaining an insight into our physical form. By doing this practice, we gain an insight into our identification with our body, thereby realizing impermanence, as well as gaining a sound relationship to our physical selves. It is also a beneficial practice where we train our mind to scan the body and direct our attention, pointedly, in one place at a time.

The Skin, Flesh, Bones Meditation

Establish a sound posture for meditation, take a few deep breaths and feel your body relaxing. Once you feel that you are in a comfortable position, begin by placing your awareness on the coming and going of the air at the tip of your nose. Let all thoughts and ideas just go by without evaluating them.

Begin the meditation by becoming aware of your skin. Scan your body from the top of your head to the tips of your toes, moving all around your body, keeping a complete focus on your outer layer. Become aware of the feeling of your clothing against your skin and the sensation experienced.

Once you have moved your awareness completely around your physical body, bring your attention to your bodies' internal organs.

Become aware of your internal organs and scan through your body systematically, as before. Start with your brain, your eyes, your tongue, your heart, spleen, kidneys, bladder, intestines, etc.. Become aware of your body tissue, your muscles, veins and the blood moving through your body.

Once you have moved your awareness completely around your physical body and back, from the feet to the crown, bring your attention to your body's skeletal system.

Become aware of your skeletal system and scan through your body systematically, as before. Start with your skull, your jaw bone, your spine, ribs, pelvic bone, the bones of the legs and arms, fingers and toes.

Once you have moved your awareness completely around your physical body and back, from the feet to the crown, bring your attention to the whole of your body once again.

Finish the meditation by resting in awareness of the experience of your skin, flesh, and bones for a few moments, before completing the meditation and reviewing your experience.

Sword and Stream Meditation

Sword and Stream meditation is a practice which combines strong focus (sword) and the free play of mind (stream). This meditation consists of two phases repeated over a number of mini-meditations, which combine to form the practice as a whole.

In the first phase of the meditation, the practitioner maintains razor sharp concentration and tries to have no thoughts. Of course, thoughts will come but these are dealt with in a particular fashion. The posture is tight, the eyes are wide and the mind is sharp.

Every time a thought or disturbing emotion arises in our awareness, we think in an instant, that the thought is cut down in one strike, as if cutting the thought with a sword.

The second phase is a conscious period of time when we allow the body to be loose and allow the mind to roam freely. All thoughts, internal chatter and ideas are welcome in this phase and fill the mind with free abandon.

Then we return back to the sword and focus once more. Through the opposites of this meditation practice, eventually the mind falls into a deep place of calm. It finds a natural calm in between two extremes.

The Sword and Stream Meditation

Establish a sound posture for meditation, take a few deep breaths and feel your body relaxing. Once you feel that you are in a comfortable position, begin by placing your awareness on the coming and going of air at the tip of your nose and let all thoughts and ideas just go by without evaluating them.

Phase one: Tighten your posture so that your back is upright, your eyes are wide, staring into space and your body feels tight. Become the sword. As soon as a thought arises in mind, do not give it a chance. Instantly, it is cut down and you remain in mind's sharp and clear natural state. Hold this stage for one to two minutes or as long as you can. Don't be too focused on cutting through and getting involved with the process, because this too is a thought. Simply cut the thought and return back to radiant awareness.

Phase two: Once you feel you can no longer hold this sharpness of mind, do the opposite. Allow your posture to become relaxed and sloppy. Your eyes can relax or close and let any thoughts flow freely in your mind. Daydream, be lazy and let your thoughts run wild in your mind.

Next, repeat phase one once more. Tighten your posture so that your back is upright, your eyes are wide, staring into space and your body feels tight. You again become the sword. As soon as a thought arises in mind, do not give it a chance. Hold this sharp awareness for as long as you can and return again to phase two.

Continue in this manner, moving from phase one to phase two for up to 10 minutes for the whole meditation. Be sure to finish on phase one and then relax into resting in mind's natural state for approximately 2 minutes.

Once you have finished the meditation, recall how you felt in each phase.

CHAPTER 11

CREATIVE VISUALIZATION MEDITATIONS

Creative visualization meditations enable us to use our minds effectively to create specific outcomes. Although visualization meditations are not limited to having our eyes closed (as some can be done with eyes open), we can use the natural tendency of our mind to create and dream by first having our eyes closed.

When we have our eyes closed, we tend to have more imagery and ideas. It is the nature of the mind to create images. For example, we may experience a memory from the past or imagine or fantasize about something or someone in the future.

Because it is quite normal for the mind to create these experiences, the following meditations give our mind something useful to do. Rather than imagining something disturbing or useless, creative visualization is a way to generate something meaningful which will help our minds.

It should be pointed out that visualization does not necessarily mean with the eyes. It is not necessary to see pictures appearing in our mind, but simply to imagine and think of the things stated in the meditation. For example, close your eyes (not now or you won't be able to read any further) and imagine your bedroom for a moment. You will probably be able to describe how your room looks. You will be able to describe where the door is, what colour the room is and where things are in relation to the shape of the room. Creative visualization meditation is no different. It is only that the subject matter is different. With practise, the subject matter becomes familiar and combined with thought, the energy of the things that we think about will follow and become our experience.

It is also important to remember that some people find visualization quite difficult. This is often because they expect too much from the meditation. The trick is to not be too hard on yourself and not build unrealistic expectations. By doing this meditation, in the same way that a body builder goes to the gym every day to build muscles, we build mental muscles to deepen our experience. This only comes through regular practise.

Purification Disc Meditation

The following meditation is a way to remove unnecessary energies in our body and mind. We all store negative impressions, either consciously or unconsciously. Everything that we have done, said and thought in this life is stored in our consciousness. The following meditation is designed to remove that which is no longer necessary for our journey.

Mentally freeing ourselves from disturbing impressions frees us emotionally, mentally, physically and spiritually. It is, therefore, a great thing to do on a regular basis.

The Purification Disc Meditation

Sit in a chair or on the floor, be comfortable and have your spine upright. A firm pillow under your bottom on a slight angle will assist in a good meditation posture. Have your eyes closed. Your chin should be slightly tucked in and hands lightly resting, palms down, on your thighs. Place your tongue on your pallet and take a moment to settle your mind with some slow breaths.

Now, place your hands in the Gassho[1] mudra, calm the mind and say silently to yourself, *"I will begin the Purification Disc Meditation now"*.

Imagine that you are sitting upon a large flat disc, much like a compact disc lying flat. Imagine that this disc is white in colour and represents the highest energy, to purify any negativity.

Now become aware of your body by scanning it from head to toe, in a similar fashion to the Zen skin, flesh, bones meditation from the previous chapter. As you scan your body, notice where you are holding tension or notice areas which feel depleted or unbalanced. You may wish to think of these areas of tension as objects residing in your body, like old junk and rubbish you do not need.

Now, focus your attention on the pure, radiant disc you are sitting upon. It is composed of a fine mesh, like a fine silk sieve, which has an ability to collect any lesser energy or problems.

As you breathe in, the disc, lying flat, rises a little up your body and as it does so, it absorbs and collects lesser energy. The disc does not fall back down on your exhale, but stays suspended in the space around your body, just a few centimetres

---

[1] Gassho is a Japanese word which means hands coming together in prayer in the middle of our chest. See the following chapter for more on this.

off the floor.

Breathe in once again and the disc again rises a few centimetres, collecting more energies or imagined objects residing in your body. Continue to breathe in and, as you do, the white disc continues to rise, collecting more and more.

As the disc rises with each inhale, it collects these unbalanced energies which may be symbolized as rubbish or junk. These sit upon the disc as it rises upwards through your body. Each inhale propels the disc slightly higher and, as it rises, it continues to collect everything which hinders your life, health and vitality.

Finally, the disc moves through the rest of your body, up through your head and comes to rest a few centimetres above the top of your head.

Feel the sense of relief that everything disturbing, harmful and unpleasant has been removed from your body and now resides upon the white disc, above your head.

Feel now, a sense of gratitude, focus on your heart. Cultivate this feeling of gratitude in your heart and as you do, imagine a fine pure light now fills the middle of your chest.

Imagine this light now rising up from your heart, along your central channel, out the top of your head and touches the disc holding the lesser energies and objects. As soon as the light touches the disc and objects, they are instantly transformed into light and filter down through the disc above our head, to melt down into our body. Imagine your body is now filled with this powerful purified energy, which energizes you completely.

Now imagine that the disc above your head dissolves into light and rest in the knowledge that everything harmful and disturbing has now been cleansed and transformed.

To complete the meditation, return your hands to the Gassho Mudra, (hands held in prayer position at heart level) and extend the wish that all the good impressions generated by doing this meditation be shared with all that lives.

Focusing Meditation

The following meditation is one method to actively transform emotions by focusing upon them and assigning a symbolic reference, thereby changing our relationship to the emotions using creative visualization and intention.

The Focusing Meditation

Sit or lie in a room, close your eyes and bring to mind a particular problem, emotion, or illness. Think about this problem and make it strong in your mind.

As you focus on this issue, ask yourself the question *"If this issue resided in my body, where would it reside?"* Then, tune into your body, to locate the root cause of this issue. Try and locate the place where you feel or sense the issue residing.

Next, think to yourself *"If this issue had a form, sensation or colour, what would it be?"* Now imagine this issue has a particular form, colour or sensation. Try and locate the place and assign it a form or symbol.

Once you have assigned the problem with a symbol form, such as a dark cloud of energy, place your hands on this area of your body and imagine a brilliant white light penetrating the issue. Imagine that this white light is reducing it in size, dissolving or extracting the problem from your body. Keep doing this until there is no sign of the issue left.

Once this issue has been removed and purified, imagine a sphere of light, or some other positive symbol which holds spiritual meaning for you and see it in the place where the issue previously resided and imagine that it is radiating light, healing and protection. This can be done throughout the day, or as needed. The more you cultivate this feeling of positive energy in this place, the less potential there is for the old problem to reoccur.

Accumulating Power Meditation

Having cleansed ourselves with the previous practice, we can develop power and protection with the following meditation.

The Accumulating Power Meditation

Imagine yourself sitting in the centre of a circle. You may wish to draw a physical circle around you before you visualize this process. The circle should be a white ring laying flat on the ground, of about three metres in diameter.

Now, focus your awareness on your heart centre. Imagine that in your heart, there is a small point of light, like a star in the night's sky, imagine dozens of similar points of light radiate outwards from this point in your heart centre.

These points of light now leap out of your body and sit on the perimeter of the circle, like the numbers on a clock, surrounding you.

Next, imagine that these points of light now turn into radiant duplicates of yourself. Imagine these are surrounding you, at the perimeter of the circle. These duplicates of yourself are beautiful, powerful and filled with energy and protection.

Take time to build these images of yourself. Once you feel happy with the images of yourself looking youthful, spiritually strong and positive, filled with every healing power, imagine these expressions of yourself moving one by one towards you, in the centre of the circle.

As each one merges with your body, feel yourself filling with their power, protection and healing energies. You are becoming their accumulated power. Continue this until all the emanations of yourself have merged with your body and you are filled with positive energy, spiritual power and protection.

To finish the meditation, rest a few moments in the experience of these energies, feeling empowered, energized and whole.

Note: You may wish to vary this meditation by imagining Buddhas around you, or a spiritual friend or teacher. Alternatively, you could imagine Reiki symbols or some other positive symbol which holds meaning for you.

Hollow Body Meditation

The hollow body meditation is a meditation on emptiness. When emptiness is described, it is not meant to represent a void or nothingness, rather, emptiness represents being free of concepts and views which cloud our mind's pure radiance. In this meditation, we utilize our imagination to visualize that within our body, there resides boundless space without any centre or limit. By doing this meditation, we will experience our mind as like a clear blue sky, unencumbered by concerns or distractions. Further practise cultivates an open and clear view of reality. We are no longer the target but instead, experience the vastness of mind's potential and free play.

The Hollow Body Meditation

Establish a sound posture for meditation, take a few deep breaths and feel your body relaxing. Once you feel that you are in a comfortable position, begin by placing your awareness on the coming and going of air at the tip of your nose and let all thoughts and ideas just go by without evaluating them.

Imagine that you are looking into and through your body. Imagine your body as not composed of flesh and blood, but transparent, clear light. Imagine that your body is completely empty. Nothing resides within you, except radiant clear space. As you go into the radiant clear space, realize that it has no beginning and therefore, no end. See or sense this light as being totally positive, expansive and representing a mirror-like wisdom of your own essential nature.

Abide a few moments in this expansive awareness. Once you feel you have meditated sufficiently on this experience of the clear light, imagine your body slowly reappearing. Bring back with you the inner knowing that you are timeless and pure, having recognized your essential nature. Abide a few moments in this knowing before ending the meditation by making wishes that whatever peace was generated during the practice be shared, for the benefit of all that lives.

Ransom Offering Meditation

The following practice is a wonderful way to clear and thereby prevent negative karmic seeds from ripening. To achieve this, we make offerings to all those whom we have harmed in the past. The more we practise this meditation, the more we change our relationship to our past deeds, as well as our view of those we have harmed.

The Ransom Offering Meditation

Think of all the harm you have caused to others, due to things that you have done, said and thought from this life and former lives. Contemplate all of the ways you have cheated, stolen or mislead others and caused them harm. How you have split up people, created discord and division as well as those you have lied to and hurt emotionally. We may not remember everything we have done from this life and certainly not from our former lives, but nevertheless, simply think that you may have wronged others and feel sorry for this.

Next, imagine these past deeds as beings residing in your body. These beings represent all those you have harmed in the past and need to repay. Make the firm resolve that you really wish to repay your harmful actions and as you do so, all of these beings spring forth from your body and now stand before you.

Imagine, with these beings standing before you, that you wish to make offerings to them. Imagine that you are giving them every kind of worldly possession. Imagine you are giving them every worldly gift.

Next, imagine that you are giving them all of your best aspirations and love and every kind word of praise and support for their journey.

Finally, imagine that you are offering even your body. Give them your organs, your blood, your life-force and see them receiving these qualities, over and over.

You now stand before them, stripped bare. Having given them everything you possess, imagine they are now truly appeased. They now smile warmly at you and all karmic debts are repaid.

This done, they return into your body, returning all of your gifts of every kind. You are left feeling empowered and whole, with a deep satisfaction that all of the things you have done in the past to harm others has now been cleansed.

Close the meditation by making the sincere wish that whatever good has just been generated from your practise will benefit all beings. Resolve from this day forth to sow only good seeds for the future.

CHAPTER 12

REIKI MUDRAS

In a similar way that we use language to communicate our words, Mudras or hand gestures communicate the language of the sub-conscious. The body and mind are intimately connected. Mudras are a direct way to cultivate energy, focus and intention for the mind.

In this chapter, we will explore a variety of Mudras which can be incorporated into Reiki practice. Each Mudra also features an accompanied meditation practice, which can be utilised alone or in conjunction with other practices.

Gassho Mudra

Figure 4. The Gassho Mudra

Of all the Mudras used in Reiki, the Gassho Mudra (figure 4) is perhaps the most widely used. The Gassho Mudra is a gesture of respect and humility. It is a Mudra which transcends both culture and religion. The Japanese word 'Gassho' means 'pressing one's hands together in prayer'.

To create the Mudra, place both of your hands together at the heart centre, in prayer position, with fingers straight. What makes this Mudra different from its Christian counterpart is its direction. The hands are not held with the fingers pointing vertical, they are pointed outwards, on an angle.

There is also a symbolic meaning for this. When we direct the hands in this way, it means that all of the energy which is generated with this Mudra is intended to be shared for both ourselves and all of humanity.

The central meaning of the Gassho Mudra represents a firm and sincere heart. Symbolically the Gassho Mudra means *"My soul bows to your soul"*, or *"The divinity in me recognizes the divinity in you"*.

This Mudra also unifies and balances the male (yang) and female (yin) energies of the body and mind and promotes right concentration. When we consider that we have active and passive sides of our body, or male and female sides, the Gassho Mudra also symbolizes the divine union of opposites. It demonstrates the divine male and the divine female in perfect union. This creates a perfect balance of wisdom (female) and active compassion (male).

As the hands are held at the centre of the body, this also represents the unity of 'Rei' - Universal Energy and 'Ki' - your vital energy. An equal number of energy centres reside above and below the heart level in the middle of our chest. The Gassho Mudra, therefore, affords the practitioner a centred place, which represents the centre of oneself and ultimately, the centre of our universe.

The Gassho Mudra is commonly used to begin and end most Reiki meditations, as a sign of focus and respect. This Mudra also represents the Reiki energy and is a way to focus our intention in mindfulness whilst meditating.

The Gassho Mudra Meditation is one of Mikao Usui's meditation practices and is today being used as part of the new Reiki techniques of the Traditional Japanese Reiki style.

This meditation practice is a passive, or 'non-doing' meditation.

The goal of the practice is to cultivate awareness in one place. Having the mind in one place enables us to truly see the true nature of our mind, unencumbered by thought that go on, day and night.

It is not that we don't notice the thoughts coming and going or try to suppress them, the idea is to not get involved with them. By doing the Gassho meditation, we can hold our mind in one place and notice the thoughts and feelings arising in mind, playing around in mind and finally returning into mind. By doing this meditation, we will begin to recognize longer periods of stillness and peace in the mind. The more this is done, the more this will become a natural state of being. All that comes and goes in the mind can be seen from the perspective of an observer.

This meditation assists in creating a calm and focused mind. Unlike many other meditations presented in this book, this practice does not incorporate any form of visualization or thought process. Ideally, one conducts the meditation by simply abiding in a mindful and aware space. One does not follow thoughts, nor listen to sounds. The focus is simply on the awareness of the Gassho Mudra and, in particular, the slight sensation of the tips of the middle fingers as they join at heart level. This meditation can be done in the morning and in the evening.

The Gassho Mudra Meditation

Sit in a chair or on the floor, be comfortable and have your spine upright. A firm pillow under your bottom on a slight angle will assist in a good meditation posture. Have your eyes closed. Your chin should be slightly tucked in and hands lightly resting palms down on your thighs. Place your tongue to your pallet and take a moment to settle your mind with some slow breaths.

Now, place your hands in the Gassho mudra, calm the mind and say silently to yourself, *"I will begin the Gassho Mudra Meditation now"*.

Keep your hands in the Gassho Mudra at heart level for the duration of the meditation. Breathe naturally and focus your mind on the point where the tips of your middle fingers meet. This slight sensation at the tips of the middle fingers is your mind's resting place. Feel your body relaxing and your mind letting go of the outside world.

Place all of your attention on the point between your middle fingers. You can even apply a slight pressure at this point, to maintain awareness. If you find your attention wandering, (which it usually does), simply bring your focus back to this point.

It is not necessary to identify with any kind of experience or sensation. Also, do not become involved in sounds, thoughts, feelings or any internal dialogue. When you notice that your mind has wandered, return it to the awareness of the slight pressure at the tips of your middle fingers.

Continue the meditation for at least 5 minutes. You can extend this practice to 10 or 20 minute sessions, but remember, it is about quality of meditation, not quantity.

End the meditation by making the wish that whatever peace was generated during the practice be shared for the benefit of all that lives.

Uttarabodhi Mudra - The gesture of supreme enlightenment.

Figure 5. The Uttarabodhi Mudra

Uttarabodhi Mudra is used for Reiki healing and for the distant remission of disease. It is a beneficial Mudra for oneself and can be used before any healing work to summon concentration, awareness and intention for healing.

A brief meditation holding this Mudra, brings a higher volume of spiritual energy into a Reiki practitioner's channels and also brings a feeling of unity and oneness.

This Mudra is also an excellent way to merge with the Reiki energy. In order to create the Mudra, the practitioner puts the two index fingers together pointing upwards, with the fingers of both hands interlaced, outward, thumbs crossed left over right. The index fingers pointing represents the element of air and the qualities of meditation, power and right effort.

The Uttarabodhi Meditation

Sit in a chair or on the floor, be comfortable and have your spine upright. A firm pillow under your bottom on a slight angle will assist in a good meditation posture. Have your eyes closed. Your chin should be slightly tucked in and hands lightly resting palms down on your thighs. Place your tongue to your pallet and take a moment to settle your mind with some slow breaths.

First, place your hands in the Gassho Mudra, calm the mind and say silently to yourself, *"I will begin the Uttarabodhi Mudra Meditation now"*.

Now, move your hands into the Uttarabodhi Mudra (see figure 5), positioned at heart level. Breathe naturally and focus your mind on the point where your index fingers point upwards. Now move the Uttarabodhi Mudra to the level of the third-eye (between your eyebrows). Close your eyes and focus your attention on your Hara for a few moments. The Hara is a place of power situated just below your navel, in the centre of your body.

Now, imagine you are breathing in through the top of your head (crown), down to your Hara on the in breath and then on the out breath, exhaling energy and light through your hands, held at the third-eye.

Continue to breathe in this way for the remainder of the meditation. With each in breath, radiant energy enters your crown, moving down to your Hara, filling it with radiant energy. With your out breath, this light ascends your central channel to your heart, shoots out in two directions down both shoulders and arms, filling your hands with pure vital energy.

Once you feel that you can no longer hold this position comfortably, descend your hands in the Uttarabodhi Mudra, to heart level.

Finally, move your hands back again to the Gassho Mudra and make the wish to share whatever good impressions have been generated, for the benefit of all.

If you are proceeding to give a Reiki treatment, this brief meditation is an excellent way to prepare your body and mind for healing. This brief Mudra meditation also brings spiritual energy into your energy channels.

Konpo-in. The balancing and stabilizing Mudra
Konpo-in is an excellent Mudra for balancing and creating stability. It increases strength of energy for hands-on healing as well as increasing the amount of Reiki energy that flows throughout the channels.

Figure 6. The Konpo-in Mudra

To form this Mudra, the two middle fingers are placed together pointing upwards, with the other fingers of both hands interlaced, and the thumbs crossed, left over right.

The middle fingers represent the element of fire and the qualities of perception, memory, patience, action and stability. Another way to think of the middle fingers, is to think of a mountain surrounded by four continents. Similar to a mandala, this Mudra is offered up to all of enlightenment. In this way, we are offering all that is fine and good to the essence of mind's perfect qualities. This brings a great richness to our minds and helps to increase generosity and to subdue selfishness.

The Konpo-in Mudra Meditation

Sit in a chair or on the floor, be comfortable and have your spine upright. A firm pillow under your bottom on a slight angle will assist in a good meditation posture. Have your eyes closed. Your chin should be slightly tucked in and hands lightly resting palms down on your thighs. Place your tongue to your pallet and take a moment to settle your mind with some slow breaths.

Now, place your hands in the Gassho Mudra, calm the mind and say silently to yourself, *"I will begin the Konpo-in Mudra Meditation now"*.

Move your hands into the Konpo-in Mudra and position the Mudra at heart level. Imagine this Mudra is a perfect offering to enlightenment. As you think this, imagine radiant white light now streaming from the Mudra and falling into your Hara, just below your navel, in the centre of your body.

With all your awareness, focus on your Hara and imagine it filling with this radiant white light. Pause a few moments to fully experience your Hara filling with this purifying energy.

Once you feel your Hara is completely filled with the energy, turn your attention to your hands. Imagine this radiant energy is increasing more and more, until it now shines outwards, in all directions in space.

As you hold this position, you may also notice energy activating in your hands.

When giving Reiki to another, we can form this Mudra until we feel the hands are ready to rest gently on the client. This Mudra increases the power and effectiveness of the treatment.

If you are doing this practice simply as a meditation, complete the practice by moving your hands back again to the Gassho Mudra and make the wish to share whatever good impressions have been generated for the benefit of all.

Naibaku ken-ni. The Mudra of Inner Bonds

Naibaku ken-ni is a Mudra which is used to help one go within for answers. It is a Mudra which creates a connection with the sub-conscious mind. With this, we gain insight into how best to facilitate a Reiki treatment, which can be applied to oneself or another in hands-on healing.

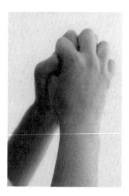

Figure 7. The Naibaku ken-ni Mudra

The Mudra is symbolic of the bodhi-heart, (the heart of unfolding) and the space between the two hands represents that which is hidden or unknown. Meditating with this Mudra enables us to summon the answers to questions. It can be used to create that which we wish to manifest in our lives and has a unifying effect on body and mind.

To form the Mudra, fingers are folded inwards towards the palm, thumbs are also tucked into the hands, touching along the side. This represents the mind and body coming together harmoniously. The thumbs symbolize spirit manifesting in two planes, with the mind represented in the left and the body in the right.

The following meditation is a way to utilize Naibaku ken-ni Mudra to evoke whatever we desire to know. With practise we can more accurately tune into what is necessary for our journey and be more aware of how to help others.

The Naibaku ken-ni Mudra Meditation

Sit in a chair or on the floor, be comfortable and have your spine upright. A firm pillow under your bottom on a slight angle will assist in a good meditation posture. Have your eyes closed. Your chin should be slightly tucked in and hands lightly resting palms down on your thighs. Place your tongue to your pallet and take a moment to settle your mind with some slow breaths.

To begin, place your hands in the Gassho Mudra, calm the mind and say silently to yourself, *"I will begin the Naibaku ken-ni Mudra Meditation now"*.

Next, move your hands into the Naibaku ken-ni Mudra, positioned at heart level. Call to mind what it is that you wish to manifest in your life, or any question you may have.

State the question or desire in the following manner, either spoken inwardly or aloud.

"I now call forth the divine right answer to my question about...(insert question or desire)"

Then repeat the affirmation a second and a third time.

Imagine that in the space between your palms, a point of light which represents your answer now forms, continuing to grow until it becomes a sphere of radiant energy. This light sphere represents the answer to your question. Of course, we usually do not know the answer right away, the purpose of this meditation is to summon our answer knowing the results will come at the right time, perhaps in a dream or an encounter in the outside world.

Now imagine that the sphere of light, which resides in between your palms held in the Naibaku ken-ni Mudra, now moves towards you and melts into your heart centre, bringing your desired result to you.

Reside a few moments in the experience of this energy.

Complete the practice by moving your hands back again to the Gassho Mudra and make the wish to share whatever good impressions have been generated, for the benefit of all.

If you are a Second Degree Reiki practitioner and have been attuned to the three Reiki symbols, you can insert the Sei Heki (the mental/emotional symbol) after the first, second and third affirmation of request. This will enhance the meditation by projecting the symbol in between the hands in the Naibaku ken-ni Mudra.

The aim of this meditation is not to have an immediate answer, although this can happen. The aim is to place your order for an answer to come. It is a little bit like placing your order at a restaurant for a meal. This practice enables you to dine at the restaurant of the universe of endless possibilities. On the menu is everything you could possibly desire. If you ask, you will receive. You just need to be patient and place your order.

CHAPTER 13

ADDITIONAL REIKI MEDITATIONS

The following meditations explore a variety of subjects, including meditations on the Reiki Symbols; The Reiki Precepts; Self-Healing Meditation and The Reiki Lineage.

Reiki Symbol Meditation

The Reiki Symbol Meditation is practiced to increase one's familiarity with the Second Degree Reiki symbols. This meditation combines visualization, breathing and mindfulness to strengthen this relationship.

Note: If you have not been attuned to the Second Degree in Reiki, you can still do this meditation just follow along as best you can.

Additional note: If you wish to view the Reiki symbols, many websites now publish them. Although it is not considered traditional to publish the Reiki symbols, you can get a sneak preview just by typing into a search engine 'Reiki Symbols'. For the purposes of up-holding traditional Reiki values, I have not provided pictures of the Reiki symbols in this book.

The Reiki Symbol Meditation

Sit in a chair or on the floor, be comfortable and have your spine upright. A firm pillow under your bottom on a slight angle will assist in a good meditation posture. Have your eyes closed. Your chin should be slightly tucked in and hands lightly resting palms down on your thighs. Place your tongue to your pallet and take a moment to settle your mind with some slow breaths.

Now place your hands in the Gassho Mudra, calm the mind and say silently to yourself, *"I will begin the Reiki Symbol Meditation now"*.

Imagine that at a comfortable distance above your head, a field of energy and light forms and gathers like clouds. Inside these clouds, begin to imagine that countless Reiki symbols appear. These are the Second Degree symbols including the Choku Rei, the Se Heki, and the Honsha Ze Shonen. They are limitless in number and all begin to pulsate with Reiki energy and light.

Now, consciously evoke the Choku Rei. In your mind state *"I now call forth all the power and energy of the Choku Rei".*

With this, countless Choku Rei symbols fall from the clouds above. Small, like raindrops, these symbols enter your body and gradually fill you, from your feet to the top of your head.

Now consciously evoke the Sei Heki. In your mind state *"I now call forth all the power and energy of the Sei Heki".*

With this, countless Sei Heki symbols fall from the clouds above. Small, like raindrops, these symbols enter your body and gradually fill you, from your feet to the top of your head.

Now consciously evoke the Honsha Ze Shonen. In your mind state *"I now call forth all the power and energy of the Honsha Ze Shonen".*

With this, countless Honsha Ze Shonen symbols fall from the clouds above. Small, like raindrops, these symbols enter your body and gradually fill you, from your feet to the top of your head.

Now, imagine that your entire body is filled with the three Reiki symbols. These symbols begin to move and dance within you. As the symbols move they give off intense rainbow coloured light, which permeates every cell of your being. Continue to imagine this for as long as you like.

To end the Meditation, place your hands in the Gassho Mudra and make the wish to share whatever good impressions have been generated, for the benefit of all.

Reiki Precepts Meditation

The Reiki Precepts Meditation is a practice to strengthen one's resolve to follow the training guidelines, as set forth by Reiki's founder Mikao Usui. Mikao Usui adopted these five admonitions from the Meiji Emperor. It is said that if one applies these into the practice of Reiki, these Precepts will bring peace of mind and happiness in this life.

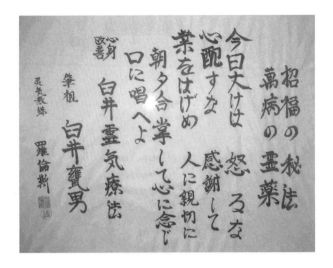

The Reiki Precepts

The secret art of inviting happiness
The miraculous medicine of all diseases
Just for today, do not anger
Do not worry and be filled with gratitude
Devote yourself to your work. Be kind to people
Every morning and evening, join your hands in prayer
Pray these words to your heart and chant these words with your mouth
Usui Reiki Treatment for the improvement of body and mind

The Reiki Precepts Meditation

Sit in a chair or on the floor, be comfortable and have your spine upright. A firm pillow under your bottom on a slight angle will assist in a good meditation posture. Have your eyes closed. Your chin should be slightly tucked in and hands lightly resting palms down on your thighs. Place your tongue to your pallet and take a moment to settle your mind with some slow breaths.

Now place your hands in the Gassho mudra, calm the mind and say silently to yourself, *"I will begin the Reiki Precepts Meditation now"*.

Next, bring your attention to the first principle *"Just for today, do not anger"*.

Recall times in your life when you were angry and times when you spoke or acted out of anger. Think how anger has caused harm to yourself and others. Now, imagine this anger as dark places in your body. Make the firm resolve not to anger in the future. In the places where you feel this anger (be it past or present), place your hands and imagine that streams of purifying Reiki energy dissolve this lower energy, until it is purified and clear.

Then, bring your attention to the second principle *"Just for today, do not worry"*.

Recall times in your life when you worried and times when you spoke or acted in a manner which caused you to lose energy by worrying about past, present or future situations.

Imagine this worry as dark places in your body. Make the firm resolve not to worry in the future. In the places where you feel worry, place your hands and imagine that streams of purifying Reiki energy are dissolving this lower energy, until it is all purified and clear.

Next, bring your attention to the third principle *"Be filled with gratitude"*.

Recall all of the things which fill you with gratitude. Consider the many gifts you bestow and the qualities which are unique to you. Consider all the ways that the spirit of gratitude has benefited yourself and others. Now, think of all your good qualities in the form of lights within your body and see these going out to touch all beings that need your help.

Then, bring your attention to the fourth principle *"Devote yourself to your work"*.

Here *work* refers to spiritual practice. Consider your spiritual path and how you might firmly place your feet upon that path. Recall the ways you have practised spiritually and generate the strong wish to cultivate aspiration for the path. Consider the results of your practise and the many ways this effort benefits yourself and others. Now, think of all your spiritual practice in the form of lights within your body and imagine these activities streaming out everywhere, touching and inspiring all beings.

Now bring your attention to the fifth principle *"Be kind to people"*. Think of the great benefit you can give to others through your actions of love, kindness, protection and compassion. Imagine that within you loving kindness radiates in all directions, it exits your body and touches all beings everywhere. They are touched by these lights and receive all the love and kindness they require.

With your hands remaining in the Gassho Mudra make the strong wish that these principles become more and more a part of you each day. End the meditation by making wishes that whatever peace was generated during these practices be shared for the benefit of all that lives.

Self-Healing Blue Sphere Meditation

The Self-Healing Blue Sphere meditation is a practice where we generate a small sphere of blue light in our heart centre. Along with the breath, the blue sphere increases in size, gradually filling up our entire body and we imagine the blue light is healing us in everyway. The blue light symbolizes healing energy. Through conscious breathing and visualization, we spread this essence throughout our entire body.

We then extend the meditation to directing the blue light to specific problem areas from the heart centre, to remove the primary causes of imbalance or illness.

The Self-Healing Blue Sphere Meditation

Sit in a chair or on the floor, be comfortable and have your spine upright. A firm pillow under your bottom on a slight angle will assist in a good meditation posture. Have your eyes closed. Your chin should be slightly tucked in and hands lightly resting palms down on your thighs. Place your tongue to your pallet and take a moment to settle your mind with some slow breaths.

Now place your hands in the Gassho Mudra, calm the mind and say silently to yourself, *"I will begin the Self-Healing Blue Sphere Meditation now"*.

Imagine that in the centre of your chest at heart level a tiny light appears, much like a small star in the night sky. This tiny point of light now begins to pulsate with energy and manifests into a small luminous blue sphere.

This blue sphere represents unlimited healing energy. Like a small spinning universe of healing energy, this sphere now begins to increase in size the more we focus upon it. As we continue to focus our attention on the blue sphere, we notice that each time we breathe in, the sphere is animated and with each out breath, the sphere increases slightly in size.

Recognizing this, we begin to become more conscious of our breath and with each inhale the sphere is animated even more and with each exhale, the blue sphere increases more and more in size (much like blowing up a blue balloon). The sphere is now much larger in the centre of our chest and blue light begins to radiate in all directions.

With each new exhale the sphere increases in size, filling our whole chest area. The blue sphere is now spreading into our throat and lower abdomen. As the sphere spreads through our body, it moves and expands into the shape of our body.

Continue to breathe in the same manner. The blue sphere continues to increase in size even more and now expands, to encompass our head and the base of our body. The more we breathe in, the more the sphere radiates light and with each exhale, the sphere increases to finally encompass our entire body and energy field. We imagine our entire body is filled from head to toe with this radiant blue light. Imagine this healing energy is within you and around you, as if you are sitting within a blue energy and light, the same shape as your body.

Sit for a few moments enjoying this healing space and circulating this healing energy throughout your entire body with your breath.

Now, focus on any areas within your body where you notice any tension, worry, illness or stress. From your heart centre, where the sphere was born, imagine this light is the most intense. From the heart centre, consciously focus that the blue light shines out and goes to these specified areas of imbalance. You can even place your hands on these areas and imagine the healing energy is flowing from the palms of your hands as well.

Continue to focus on these problem areas and move from one to the next, until you feel the healing is complete.

Become aware of your whole body once more, feeling the deep relief that the meditation has assisted your body and mind in its healing process. The blue light now disappears and our habitual self is now present, but something has changed. We are now a perfect embodiment of health, vitality and peace.

To end the Meditation, place your hands in the Gassho Mudra and make the wish to share whatever good impressions have been generated, for the benefit of all.

Usui Meditation

The following meditation serves as a way to acknowledge our connection to the founder of Reiki, Mikao Usui. Here, we imagine that we meet Usui. Through the act of giving and receiving imagined gifts, we generate a positive aspiration and strengthen our connection to the Reiki lineage.

Figure 8. Mikao Usui

The Usui Meditation

Sit in a chair or on the floor, be comfortable and have your spine upright. A firm pillow under your bottom on a slight angle will assist in a good meditation posture. Have your eyes closed. Your chin should be slightly tucked in and hands lightly resting palms down on your thighs. Place your tongue to your pallet and take a moment to settle your mind with some slow breaths.

Now place your hands in the Gassho Mudra, calm the mind and say silently to yourself, *"I will begin the Usui Meditation now"*.

Begin the meditation by imagining that you are walking along a path in a beautiful forest. As you walk along the path, you come over a rise and see before you a beautiful temple. The temple is ancient and peaceful. As you approach the temple, the doors open. You walk inside and standing opposite you is a wall with a large wooden door. The door has light streaming out from between the corners and you feel compelled to enter.

As you approach the door, you see the words 'Mikao Usui' written as a plaque above the door. Go up to the door, push on it and you find it effortlessly opens. You now enter the room and see Usui standing there before you. He is standing before you in a single white robe, his eyes are smiling at you and he gestures for you to approach him.

In the room between yourself and Usui is a box containing a gift for Usui. This gift may be a material or a symbolic gift. There may also be something that you wish to say to honour Usui and his tradition. You open this box and see what is inside.

Bestow this gift to Usui Sensei. Usui receives this gift and is most grateful. In return, Usui has something for you. This time, he presents you with a gift. Allow whatever you imagine to flow out of the meditation. This may be an object, a Reiki Attunement, an acknowledgement or a message.

Once you have received this gift, give thanks to Usui and make the promise to uphold and honour his tradition. As a sign of his love and respect for you, he bows deeply. In return you bow. It is now time to leave. You turn to face the door you entered, then walk into the main hall of the temple and back on the path, carrying with you your gift from Usui.

To end the Meditation, place your hands into the Gassho Mudra and make the wish to share whatever good impressions have been generated, for the benefit of all.

CHAPTER 14

JAPANESE REIKI MEDITATIONS

Reiki Undo Meditation

Reiki Undo Meditation is a practice which comes from the sixth president of the Usui Reiki Ryoho Gakkai, Ms. Koyama. This exercise assists with the release of stress and tension in the body. It is also a way to de-armour the body of fixed energy patterns or rigid thinking. A literal translation of Reiki Undo is 'spiritual energy exercise'. Undo means 'motion, exercise'.

As this meditation introduces movement, it is best to have a space for the practice where you will be able to move freely. It is ideal to remove any furniture with sharp edges to the side, so you have plenty of space to move with the energy of Reiki. It is best to allow up to 10 minutes for this practice.

The Reiki Undo Meditation

Stand comfortably in the centre of the room. Open your eyes and breathe steadily and easily. Place your hands in the Gassho Mudra, calm your mind and say silently, *"I will begin the Reiki Undo Meditation now"*.

Begin the meditation by reaching your hands above your head and connect to the fullness of the Reiki energy. (You can imagine your body filling with energy). Imagine that you are touching a vast field of energy and light.

Once you have made this connection to the energy, slowly move your hands down your body with your palms facing you. In the same way water fills a vessel, imagine that as your hands descend, the Reiki energy is merging with your energy field and body. Your hands move to the sides of your body, fingers relaxed. Feel your breath flowing naturally and slowly and drop your awareness to your Hara and relax.

Now connect with your breath. As you breathe in, begin to release all the stress and tension from your body. On the out breath, let it go completely.

Your body may begin to move after a few of these releasing breaths. Don't force it, just allow, relax and let go. Imagine that the Reiki energy is completely filling your body. The more you breathe, the more you begin to let go and surrender to the Reiki energy moving through your body.

Once you feel this connection, allow your body to move in any way you feel inclined. Trust in this flow and move as Reiki energy. Remember, it is not you who is moving your body, it is the Reiki energy moving your body on your behalf. Let go and give yourself over to the flow of Reiki.

Your movements may be small, they may be dramatic, they may look like 'Tai Chi' or dynamic and energetic. Whichever way the Reiki energy moves your body is right for you in this moment.

Once your body has come to a standstill, place your hands back into the Gassho Mudra and give thanks to the Reiki energy for its healing.

To finish, you can also shake your hands to the sides of your body, up and down and back and forth. (This releases any unused energy or congestion as a result of this practice).

It is suggested that you should practice this technique every day for a period of three months. The more you practice this technique, the more you will be able to let go and the more 'in flow' you will become with the Reiki energy.

This practice can also begin to affect you on other levels. When you think about it, the more in flow you are with Reiki, the more you will flow with life.

Kenyoku-ho Meditation

This meditation technique helps to cleanse and enhance your energy field, whilst disconnecting you from outside influences. This technique specifically cleanses the inner organs, as well as being an excellent way to cleanse the body of unwanted energy.

A literal translation of Kenyoku is 'dry bath'. Ken means, 'drought, dry, drink up, heaven, or emperor'; Yoku means, 'bathe, be favored with, or bask in'; and *ho* means, 'technique, method or way'. This is an original technique from Mikao Usui.

In addition to the outer form, I have added a visualization process which can be introduced into this practice. As illustrated with the images that follow, one sweeps the body and arms, combining the breath and intention to remove unwanted energy.

Figure 9. The Kenyoku-ho strokes down the body and arms.

The Kenyoku-ho Meditation:
Sit or stand comfortably. Place your hands into the Gassho Mudra, calm your mind and say silently to yourself *'I will begin Kenyoku-ho Meditation now"*.

Place your right hand fingertips near the top of your left shoulder (where the collarbone and shoulder meet). Your hand is flat with your palm toward your body.

In one motion, move your hand downward in a diagonal line, from the left shoulder to the right hip and flick off. (Take in a breath before each sweep, as this assists with releasing excess energy from your energy field.)

Repeat the movements with the left hand to the right side of the body in the same way. Move your left hand in a downward diagonal line from the right shoulder to the left hip.

Repeat this once again on the left shoulder. (Twice on the left hand side and once on the right hand side).

Now place your right hand on the left upper arm or shoulder, with your palm facing down. Your hand should be flat with your fingers pointing outwards. In one motion, move the right hand down the arm to the finger tips and flick off. Shake your hand to release excess energy if desired.

Repeat this motion now for the right arm, with your left hand moving down your right arm to the finger tips and flick off as before.

Repeat this once more for the left arm. (Twice on the left hand side and once on the right hand side).

Now that you have the sequence of the outer form, the following visualization can be incorporated.

The Visualization for Kenyoku-ho
Before beginning the practice, place your hands in Gassho and focus your

awareness on your body. Sense any areas of imbalance and imagine these as dark points in the organs of your body.

When you begin the sweeping across the body, imagine that you are wearing a white glove on each hand.

As you make the sweep across the body and arms, the white glove collects all these dark points, which accumulate on the gloves as black soot.

When the hands flick off to the sides of the body, all this negativity leaves your body and the glove and falls to the ground, transformed into diamonds, sapphires, rubys and pearls. Each time you sweep, you are removing negativity from the internal organs, as well as removing unwanted energy from your arms and palms.

Be sure to transform the lower energies into symbols of clarity, beauty and light (i.e. precious stones, stars of light, mantras etc...)

At the end of the exercise, imagine that all of these lights or precious stones return back into your body, via the soles of your feet. Alternatively, you can think of all those you may have harmed or stolen from in the past and that all these precious items go to them. This way we repay old karmic debts.

To finish the meditation, place your hands back into the Gassho Mudra and make the wish to share whatever good impressions have been generated, for the benefit of all.

Reiki Mawashi Meditation

Reiki Mawashi is a popular Japanese Reiki technique which is traditionally performed in a group setting and means 'The traditional method of Reiki circle' or 'Reiki current'.

This technique helps to sensitize the Practitioner to feel energy flow and to sensitize the hands for healing.

To do Reiki Mawashi, a group of Reiki practitioners make a circle and hold hands. This allows a Reiki current to flow from the palms. The word Mawashi means 'round, game, revolve, or current'. This technique comes from Mr. Horoshi Doi.

Although this technique is usually performed in a group setting, Reiki Mawashi can also be done as a solo practice.

The following meditation I have developed for my students who wanted to practise the technique but had little opportunity when practising outside the institute's clinic times.

The Reiki Mawashi for One Meditation

When practising 'Reiki Mawashi for One,' we utilize the left and right sides of the body to give and receive Reiki. Here, the right side symbolizes 'giving' and the left 'receiving'.

Sit in a chair or on the floor, be comfortable and have your spine upright. A firm pillow under your bottom on a slight angle will assist in a good meditation posture. Have your eyes closed. Your chin should be slightly tucked in and hands lightly resting palms down on your thighs. Place your tongue to your pallet and take a moment to settle your mind with some slow breaths.

Now, place your hands in the Gassho Mudra, calm the mind and say silently to yourself, *"I will begin the Reiki Mawashi Meditation now"*.

Figure 10. Reiki Mawashi Mudra – Solo hand positions

Bring your hands into the Reiki Mawashi Mudra and position this at heart level (figure 10.) Your right hand is held above and your left hand is held below. The hands are held in this position, as if holding a ball between your palms.

Imagine that in the middle of your chest a fine point of light emerges. As you focus upon this point of light, it increases in size to form a small sphere of radiant energy.

Next, imagine this sphere divides (just in the same way cells divide) and imagine that a second sphere emerges from the first. Now two radiant spheres reside in your heart, each both perfect and pure.

Breathe in deeply and with your exhale, imagine the second sphere (which came from the first) gently moves from your heart centre and travels along your right shoulder and down your right arm. By the end of the exhale, this sphere comes to a resting place between your cupped hands in front of you. This sphere is hovering in the space between your hands.

On your next inhale, imagine radiant light from the sphere between your hands is received from the left hand, streams up your left arm and melts into the remaining sphere in your heart centre. On your exhale, this light now pours from the sphere in your heart and streams down your right arm, exits your right palm and melts into the sphere in between your hands.

Again on your next inhale, imagine radiant light from the sphere between your hands now pours from this sphere and is received from the left hand, streams up your left arm and melts into the sphere in your heart centre. Again on your exhale, this light pours from the sphere in your heart and streams down your right arm and into the sphere between your palms.

Continue this movement of energy in conjunction with the breath for as long as you feel comfortable. As you continue to meditate in this fashion, you can also imagine that the longer you practise, the more the energy fields between your palms and heart centre increases.

Figure 11. Reiki Mawashi Mudra – Hands on heart position

Once you feel you would like to end the practice, bring your hands together and move them to your heart centre (figure 11). As you do, imagine the two spheres (the one between your hands and the one in your heart centre) melt into one another.

Holding your palms to your heart centre, imagine that these spheres now dissolve and the radiant energy continues to fill your entire body.

To finish the meditation, place your hands back into the Gassho Mudra and make the wish to share whatever good impressions have been generated, for the benefit of all.

CHAPTER 15

FURTHER JAPANESE REIKI MEDITATIONS

The Hikari no Kokyu-ho Meditation

Sit in a chair or on the floor, be comfortable and have your spine upright. A firm pillow under your bottom on a slight angle will assist in a good meditation posture. Have your eyes closed. Your chin should be slightly tucked in and hands lightly resting palms down on your thighs. Place your tongue to your pallet and take a moment to settle your mind with some slow breaths.

Now, place your hands in the Gassho Mudra, calm the mind and say silently to yourself: *"I will begin Hikari no Kokyu-ho now"*.

Reach your hands high above your head and connect to the fullness of the Reiki energy. Imagine that you are touching a vast field of energy and light, which then fills your body.

Once you have made this connection, slowly move your hands down your body with the palms facing you. In the same way as water fills a vessel, imagine that as

Figure 12. Connecting to the Reiki energy above the crown and merging the
Reiki energy into and through the body.

your hands descend, the Reiki energy is merging with your energy field and body.
Move your hands back to your lap, palms down and fingers relaxed. Feel your
breath flowing naturally and slowly, and drop your awareness to your Hara.

While breathing in, imagine that the light of Reiki is entering your crown
chakra from the field of energy above. Imagine this energy moving down your
central channel, to your Hara, all the while expanding, until your whole body is
filled with Reiki Energy. Imagine that this light is dissolving all tensions, stress,
disease, negative thoughts and emotions.

On the out breath, imagine the light of Reiki is expanding beyond your skin
and filling your aura in every direction. (This breathing technique can gradually be
drawn out to extended breathing cycles).

As you are breathing, maintain your awareness on being filled with the Reiki
energy and on the out breath, expand this energy outwards. Here, the breath
becomes an anchor for the practice, as you incorporate the visualization to the best
of your ability.

Once you feel complete, imagine the Reiki energy field above condenses in
space. It now dissolves into light, which rains down upon you. You then become
all of the power of Reiki, inseparable from this essence.

Sit a few moments in the essence of the Reiki energy. To finish the meditation,
place your hands back in the Gassho Mudra and make the wish to share whatever
good impressions have been generated, for the benefit of all.

Gassho Kokyu-ho Meditation
(Breathing through the Hands)
This meditation is a practice to establish and increase the pathways of Reiki energy through the hands. It is also a method to sensitize the hands for healing. This technique assists in clearing your mind and connecting you to higher levels of consciousness, whilst remaining grounded. With ongoing use, Gassho Kokyu-ho will increase your ability to channel Reiki energy. A literal translation of Gassho Kokyu-ho is 'hand breathing'. Gassho means 'pressing one's hands together in prayer'; *Kokyu* means, 'breath, or respiration'; and *ho* means, 'technique, method or way'. This is an original technique from Mikao Usui and additional instructions for a visualization process are presented here following this meditation to purify negativity.

The Gassho Kokyu-ho Meditation
Sit in a chair or on the floor, be comfortable and have your spine upright. A firm pillow under your bottom on a slight angle will assist in a good meditation posture. Have your eyes closed. Your chin should be slightly tucked in and hands lightly resting palms down on your thighs. Place your tongue to your pallet and take a moment to settle your mind with some slow breaths.

Now place your hands in the Gassho Mudra, calm the mind and say silently to yourself *"I will begin Gassho Kokyu-ho now"*.

Reach your hands high above your head and connect to the fullness of the Reiki energy. Imagine that you are touching a vast field of energy and light, which then fills your body.

Once you have made this connection, slowly move your hands down your body with palms facing you. In the same way as water fills a vessel, imagine that as your hands descend, the Reiki energy is merging with your energy field and body. Move your hands back to your lap, palms down and fingers relaxed. Feel your breath flowing naturally and slowly and drop your awareness to your Hara.

Once you have made this connection, slowly move your hands back to Gassho Mudra position.

With your hands in the Gassho Mudra, imagine in the space in front of you, a sphere of energy and light forms. This is roughly the size of a basketball. Imagine this sphere in the colour blue and imagine the tips of your fingers are just inside this bubble of healing energy.

Now begin to imagine that you are breathing through your hands. While breathing in, imagine Reiki energy entering your hands from the sphere in front of you, the blue light streaming down both your arms and meeting in your upper chest. From here, it flows down your central channel, to your Hara. Feel this light expanding until the Hara is filled with energy.

On the out breath, imagine the light moving from the Hara back along the same pathway to the hands and filling them with energy. This energy is then released into the hands, radiating vital energy out in all directions.

With practise, you may feel a strong presence in your palms, such as a tingling or pulsing sensation. Like the previous meditation, this breathing technique can gradually be drawn out to extended breathing cycles.

Repeat the meditation for as long as you like. Once you feel this is complete, imagine the blue field of energy and light condenses in space and merges completely with your hands, filling them with healing energy.

Alternative Gassho Kokyu-ho Practice for Purification.
This technique was created by the author.

The Gassho Kokyu-ho Meditation (alternative meditation)
Once you have consciously made a connection with the Reiki energy, proceed with the following stages.

Imagine all of your illness, stress and tension congregate in your Hara. These manifest as black smoke.

Begin to imagine that you are breathing through your hands. Whilst breathing in, imagine Reiki energy is entering your hands from the sphere in front of you. This time the energy is white in colour (for purification) and is now streaming down both arms meeting in your upper chest and flowing down your central channel, down to your Hara.

Imagine this light expands until the Hara is filled with Reiki energy. It now stirs up our negativity (the black smoke) as the light comes in.

On the out breath, imagine that you are breathing out all of the black smoke and light. This is moving from the Hara back along the same pathway to the hands. This negativity now leaves the body via the hands, into the sphere in front of you.

The field of energy and light instantly transforms your negativity (the black smoke) into more healing energy. Continue to breathe in more purifying energy from the sphere in front of you.

Repeat the meditation for as long as you like. Once you feel that all the black smoke has been transformed, continue to breathe in the light, in and out.

Once you feel this is complete, imagine that the field of energy and light condenses in space and merges completely with your hands and fills them with healing energy.

Sit a few moments in the essence of the Reiki energy. To finish the meditation, make the wish to share whatever good impressions have been generated, for the benefit of all.

Chakra Kassei Kokyu-ho Meditation
(Breathing through the Chakras)

Chakra Kassei Kokyu-ho meditation is a technique that sends Reiki energy throughout the whole body and activates the chakras. This meditation also opens and clears the central channel, base, heart, and crown chakras.

A literal translation of Chakra Kassei Kokyu-ho is 'breathing method to activate the chakras'. Kassei means, 'active or activate'; Kokyu means, 'breath, respiration'; and ho means, 'technique, method or way'. This meditation comes from Mr. Hiroshi Doi, a member of the Usui Reiki Ryoho Gakkai (Reiki learning Society).

In addition to the outer form, I have added a visualization process which can be introduced into the practice.

The Chakra Kassei Kokyu-ho Meditation

Figure 13. This is the basic pattern for the hands held in the Gassho Mudra for the Chakra Kassei Kokyu-ho Meditation.

Sit in a chair or on the floor, be comfortable and have your spine upright. A firm pillow under your bottom on a slight angle will assist in a good meditation posture. Have your eyes closed. Your chin should be slightly tucked in and hands lightly resting palms down on your thighs. Place your tongue to your pallet and take a moment to settle your mind with some slow breaths.

Now place your hands in the Gassho Mudra, calm the mind and say silently to yourself *"I will begin Chakra Kassei Kokyu-ho Meditation now"*.

Following the movement of the hands as per the photos featured (figure 13), begin from the base Chakra on the in breath, up to the heart centre. On the exhale, extend your hands in the Gassho Mudra position in front of you. On the next inhale, bring your hands, still in the Gassho Mudra, back to touch your heart centre. With the next exhale, extend your hands in the Gassho Mudra high above your head.

On the next inhale, move your hands from the top of your head once again to the heart centre. Then exhale and extend your hands out in front once more. Again inhale and draw your hands in the Gassho Mudra back to your heart centre. Lastly, exhale moving our hands in the Gassho Mudra back to your base chakra.

The hands continue to move in this way whilst in the Gassho Mudra. This represents the movement of healing energy. The sequence just described represents the outer form and you can incorporate the following visualization as best you can.

The Chakra Kassei Kokyu-ho Visualization

Before you begin the practice, focus your attention inwardly. Imagine that above your head is a white ball of Reiki energy. Also, imagine in front of your heart centre a second ball manifests and at the base of your body a third. All three spheres are linked by your central channel.

Next, imagine that as you breathe in (as per the breathing pattern), white light is being drawn up from the sphere at the base of your body, up your central channel to your heart centre.

On your exhale, imagine any purified energies now pour out of your heart centre into the sphere before you, as billowing black smoke.

Inhale, imagining you are drawing pure healing energies into your heart centre. Exhale now, imagining that any purified energies pour out of your crown centre, into the sphere above you, as billowing black smoke.

On your in breath, imagine you are drawing in healing energies from the sphere above you, down into your heart centre. On your exhale, imagine any purified energies now pour out of your heart centre, into the sphere before you.

Inhale now, imagining that you are drawing healing energies into your heart centre and on your exhale, imagine any purified energies now pour out of your base chakra, into the sphere below you as black smoke.

This is one round of the visualized sequence.

Continue to breathe and visualize this sequence for as long as you like. The longer you meditate in one session, the less dense the black smoke becomes. This is because the spheres above, in front and below are transforming impure energy from your body. Eventually, only radiant light will come and go with the breath.

To end the Meditation, with your hands remaining in the Gassho Mudra, make the wish to share whatever good impressions have been generated, for the benefit of all.

Note: You can also extend this practice to other energy centres, such as the Hara, solar plexus, throat and third eye. In this case, maintain the meditation as usual, the only changes being the places where the sphere manifests before you. If, for example, you choose to work on your speech centre (throat), imagine a sphere manifests in front of your throat. Ideally, you should do at least three visualized cycles at each centre and more is always desirable.

However, as this particular meditation has a powerful effect on the whole energy system, it is recommended not to extend your practice any longer than 15 minutes in any one sitting. These meditation sessions can be drawn out to longer periods over time. You may feel somewhat 'spacey' after doing this meditation, so it is best to take a break, drink some water or eat some food before driving a car.

Reiki Shower Meditation

Reiki Shower is a meditation technique for showering yourself in Reiki energy. This meditation cleanses the body and increases vital energy and is also an excellent way to cleanse your energy field (Aura) of lower or unwanted energies.

This meditation comes from Reiki Master, Walter Lübeck. Reiki Shower is a practice which can address the energy cause of illness. Just in the same way that the Kenyoku-ho meditation assists in cleaning the internal organs, the Reiki Shower meditation assists in removing diseased energy which may be contributing to illness anddisease in the physical body.

This is based on the notion that all illness, before it manifests on the physical, first forms in the energy body. One can readily perceive this when scanning the aura over a physical aliment or injury. Just as there is a noticeable imbalance in the body, so too is there a discharge of lower energy, which forms much like clouds of congested energy above the area of imbalance.

The Reiki Shower Meditation
Sit in a chair or on the floor, be comfortable and have your spine upright. A firm pillow under your bottom on a slight angle will assist in a good meditation posture. Have your eyes closed. Your chin should be slightly tucked in and hands lightly resting palms down on your thighs. Place your tongue to your pallet and take a moment to settle your mind with some slow breaths.

Now place your hands in the Gassho Mudra, calm the mind and say silently to yourself *"I will begin Reiki Shower practice now"*.

Reach your hands high above your head and connect to the fullness of the Reiki energy. Imagine that you are touching a vast field of energy and light, which now fills your body.

Once you have made this connection, slowly move your hands down your body with palms facing you. In the same way as water fills a vessel, imagine that as your hands descend, the Reiki energy merges with your energy field and body. Move your hands back to your lap with palms down and fingers relaxed. Feel your breath flowing naturally and slowly, and drop your awareness to your Hara.

With your next in breath, bring your hands up the sides of your body with your palms facing the sky and on your exhale, wash your hands over your body (not touching) with downwards strokes towards the ground. Feel the fullness of this energy and slowly move your hands down the front of your body with your palms facing you. Your hands are bathing you in Reiki energy, cleansing all areas of imbalance and purifying all disease, negative emotions and thoughts. All these lower energies are transmuted or seen moving down your body and out the soles of your feet, never to return.

Imagine the earth beneath you cracks open slightly, absorbing the lower energies and excess Reiki energy. Feel this energy flowing over you. As it does, it takes with it all these lower energies down into the earth where they are transformed by the power of nature.

If you have an area in particular which requires more time, spend as much time as is necessary bathing this area.

On the next in breath, bring your hands once again out to the sides of your body and as you breathe in, imagine you are drawing in more purifying energy over your head. Now on your out breath, wash your hands over your body again.

Continue this for several minutes or until you feel purified and cleansed of any lower energies. Once you feel that you are full of positive healing energy, return your hands to the Gassho Mudra. Imagine that the earth below you seals up once again and you are left feeling pure and clear.

Now, imagine that your body becomes tight and all of the openings are sealed. Like a vessel being filled with water, imagine your body is being filled with Reiki energy. The Reiki energy continues to rain down through the top of your head, filling you completely, until it overflows out the top of your head.

To finish, make the wish to share whatever good impressions have been generated, for the benefit of all.

Note: This is an excellent meditation to do under a waterfall or in the shower. Imagine the water is the Reiki energy and that it not only moves over your body but through it, cleaning all areas of imbalance.

Spinal Breathing (Sekizui Joka Ibuki-ho) Meditation

A meditation on cleansing the spinal cord with the breath.

The following meditation is designed to remove accumulated impressions, which are stored in our body and in particular, energies along the spine. According to the spiritual practices of Koshin-do, the spinal cord records and stores negative actions from a person's life. Using the following meditation, these negative energies from the past can be cleared and purified, thus replacing the individual with positive life force energy. This method also enlivens the cells of the body.

The Spinal Breathing (Sekizui Joka Ibuki-ho) Meditation

Sit in a chair or on the floor, be comfortable and have your spine upright. A firm pillow under your bottom on a slight angle will assist in a good meditation posture. Have your eyes closed. Your chin should be slightly tucked in and hands lightly resting palms down on your thighs. Place your tongue to your pallet and take a moment to settle your mind with some slow breaths.

Place your hands in the Gassho Mudra, calm the mind and say silently to yourself *"I will begin the Sekizui Joka Ibuki-ho Meditation now"*.

Now reach your hands high above your head and connect to the fullness of the Reiki energy. Imagine that you are touching a vast field of energy and light, which then fills your body.

Once you have made this connection, slowly move your hands down your body with palms facing you. In the same way as water fills a vessel, imagine that as your hands descend, the Reiki energy merges with your energy field and body. Move your hands back to your lap with palms down and fingers relaxed. Feel your breath flowing naturally and slowly, and drop your awareness to your Hara.

Visualize your backbone as a long pipe, from the base of your spine to the top of your head. Below your coccyx, at the base of your spine, imagine there resides a clear pool of purifying water. This clear pool represents purifying and cleaning energies which harmonise and balance your body and mind.

Imagine that you have an ability to perceive the inside of this pipe which runs along your spine and that you can perceive your past harmful actions. Imagine that these have attached to the inside of the pipe, in the form of dirt and grime.

As if sucking up water from a straw, with the in breath, imagine that purifying water from this pool now rises up from the base of your body, travelling up your spine pipe, to the top of your head. This purifying water travels over the crown to your third eye, in the centre of your forehead.

On the exhale, breathe out, making the sound 'ahh'. The vibration of the 'ahh' sound shakes the pipe along with the water exiting the base of the body and releases all of the negativity collected.

On the in breath, imagine more clear water from the pool below moving up the pipe from the coccyx to the third eye. Imagine that the pipe is filled with this pure water.

On the out breath, along with the long 'ahh' sound, all the water flows out the base of your body, removing any impurities from your system.

Repeat this process in your own time, over and over again.

Once this feels complete, meditate in silence and focus your awareness on your third eye noticing how this now feels.

Next, imagine you are breathing through your skin, so that your whole body becomes filled with Reiki energy. With every in breath, imagine that you are drawing in life force energy from all directions, into your body. With each exhale, this vital energy expands within and around you in all directions. Continue meditating like this for a few minutes.

Once you feel that you are now full of positive healing energy, return your hands to the Gassho Mudra and finish by wishing that all the good impressions that have just been generated, be shared for the benefit of all that lives.

Gassho Meditation

The Gassho Meditation is one of Mikao Usui's meditation practices and is today being used as part of the new Reiki techniques of the traditional Japanese Reiki style.

This meditation practice is a passive or 'non-doing' meditation.

The goal of the practice is to cultivate awareness in one place. Having the mind in one place enables us to see the true nature of our mind.

It is not that we don't notice the thoughts coming and going or try to suppress them, the idea is not to get involved with them. By doing the Gassho meditation, we can hold our mind in one place and notice the thoughts and feelings arising in mind, playing around in mind and finally returning into mind. By doing this meditation we will begin to recognize longer periods of stillness and peace in the mind. The more this is done, the more this will become a natural state of being. All that comes and goes in the mind can be seen from the perspective of an observer.

To do this meditation, place your hands in the Gassho Mudra.

Figure 14. The Gassho Mudra

This meditation assists in creating a calm and focused mind. Unlike many other meditations presented in this book, this practice does not incorporate any form of visualization or thought process. Ideally, one conducts the meditation by simply abiding in a mindful and aware space. One does not follow thoughts, nor listen to sounds. The focus is simply on the awareness of the Gassho Mudra and in particular, the slight sensation of the tips of the middle fingers as they join at heart level. This meditation can be done in the morning and in the evening.

The Gassho Mudra Meditation

Sit in a chair or on the floor, be comfortable and have your spine upright. A firm pillow under your bottom on a slight angle will assist in a good meditation posture. Have your eyes closed. Your chin should be slightly tucked in and hands lightly resting palms down on your thighs. Place your tongue to your pallet and take a moment to settle your mind with some slow breaths.

Now, place your hands in the Gassho Mudra, calm the mind and say silently to yourself, *"I will begin the Gassho Meditation now"*.

Keep your hands in the Gassho Mudra at heart level for the duration of the meditation. Breathe naturally and focus your mind on the point where the tips of your middle fingers meet. This slight sensation at the tips of the middle fingers is your mind's resting place. Feel your body relaxing and your mind letting go of the outside world.

Place all of your attention on the point between your middle fingers. You can even apply a light pressure at this point to maintain awareness. If you find your attention wandering, (which it usually does), simply bring your focus back to this point.

It is not necessary to identify with any kind of experience or sensation. Also, do not become involved in sounds, thoughts, feelings or any internal dialogue. When you notice that your mind has wandered, return it to the awareness of the light pressure at the tips of your middle fingers.

Continue the meditation for at least 5 minutes. You can also extend this practice in time to 10 or 20 minutes. Remember, it is about quality of meditation, not quantity.

End the meditation by making wishes that whatever peace was generated during the practice be shared for the benefit of all that lives.

BIBLIOGRAPHY

The Words of my Perfect Teacher by Patrul Rinpoche
How to Meditate by Kathleen McDonald
Luminous Mind by Kalu Rinpoche
Buddhism Today, Volumes 1, 12 and 13.
Modern Reiki Method for Healing by Hiroshi Doi

Further Reading

The titles presented here are but a few of the more useful books on Reiki that I have found useful.

Reiki - Penelope Quest - Piatkus
Reiki: The healing touch - William Lee Rand - Vision Publications
Reiki: Way of the Heart - Walter Lübeck - Lotus Press
Reiki for First Aid - Walter Lübeck - Lotus Press
The Complete Reiki Handbook - Walter Lübeck - Lotus Press
Reiki Fire - Frank Arjava Petter - Lotus Press
Reiki: the Legacy of Dr. Usui - Frank Arjava Petter - Lotus Press
The Original Reiki Handbook of Dr. Mikao Usui - Frank Arjaya Petter - Lotus Press
Reiki and the Seven Chakras - Richard Ellis - Vermillion
Modern Reiki Method for Healing - Hiroshi Doi - Fraser Journal Publishing
The Spirit of Reiki: A complete handbook of the Reiki System - Petter, Rand, Lübeck - Lotus Press.
Reiki for Beginners - David F. Vennells - Llewellyn
Reiki Mastery - David F. Vennells - O-Books Publishing
Reiki Systems of the World - Oliver Klatt - Lotus Press
The Reiki Source Book - Frans and Bronwen Stiene - O-Books Publishing
The Japanese Art of Reiki - Frans and Bronwen Stiene - O-Books Publishing
Reiki: The essential guide to the ancient healing art - Chris & Penny

Parkes - Vermillion

15 Minute Reiki - Chris & Penny Parkes - Thorsons

Reiki Jin Kei Do - Steve Gooch - O-Books Publishing

Empowerment through Reiki - Paula Horan - Lotus Press

The Complete Book of Traditional Reiki - Amy Z. Rowland - Healing Arts Press

Recommended Reiki Websites

The Internet is a wealth of information however it is good to know where to go in that vast ocean. The following are a list of recommended websites that cover an array of information about Reiki.

www.reikitraining.com.au *The International Institute for Reiki Training*

www.reiki.org *The International Centre for Reiki Training*

www.usui-do.org *Usui – Do*

www.reikialliance.com *The Reiki Alliance*

www.trtia.org *The Radiance Technique*

www.reiki.net.au *The International House of Reiki*

www.angelfire.com/az/SpiritMatters/contents.html *Reiki Ryoho Pages*

www.reikidharma.com *Reiki Site of Frank Arjava Petter*

www.angelreiki.nu *Reiki Plain and Simple*

www.threshold.ca *Reiki Threshold*

www.reiki-evolution.co.uk *Reiki Evolution*

www.healing-touch.co.uk *Healing Touch – Reiki Jin Kei Do*

www.australianreikiconnection.com.au *The Australian Reiki Connection*

http://reiki.7gen.com *The Reiki Page*

www.reiki-magazin.de *German Reiki Magazine*

ABOUT THE AUTHOR

Lawrence Ellyard is the Founder and Director of the International Institute for Reiki Training and is the best selling author of *'Reiki Healer'* and *'Reiki 200 Questions and Answers for Beginners'*. Lawrence Ellyard is based in Byron Bay, Northern New South Wales, Australia.

'Reiki Meditations for Beginners' is his seventh book.

About the IIRT

The International Institute for Reiki Training offers traditional Japanese Reiki Training and is regarded as one of the foremost training institutes for Reiki in the world today. The IIRT has conducted international training programs for exisiting Reiki Practitioners and Masters, offering classes in Europe, the United Kingdom, The United Sates, Australia and New Zealand. For more information about the Institute visit: www.reikitraining.com.au

About our Website

On our site you will find over 100 pages, covering everything there is to know about Reiki. Our site is globally one of the most comprehensive and contains details on the classes we offer, as well as Reiki history; Reiki news; Membership opportunities; Online Practitioner Directory, and details of where classes are held.

If you would like to contact Lawrence Ellyard or the Institute simply contact us from the website or write to us at:

The International Institute for Reiki Training
PO Box 733 Byron Bay, NSW 2481 Australia.